London and Docklands Walks
Professor S K Al Naib

15. NEW CRANE WHARF

Built in 1873 at the junction of Wapping High Street and Wapping Wall, this conversion is a good example of mixed use, with flats, commercial units and shops. Metropolitan Wharf, next door, has been converted to house some 150 small firms.

16. WAPPING WALL

So named after the tidal defences built in 1570-71, when the area first came into serious maritime use.

17. HYDRAULIC PUMPING STATION

This took water from the dock, coal from Shadwell Basin next door, created steam in six boilers and stored hydraulic energy in two accumulator towers - which then drove the engines at Tower Bridge to raise and lower the bridge, as well as - amongst other things - the safety curtain at the London Palladium.

20. KING EDWARD VII MEMORIAL PARK

Opened in 1922, this riverside garden offers good views of Rotherhithe and the Isle of Dogs. A brick built cupola disguises a ventilation shaft for the Rotherhithe Tunnel.

24. LIMEHOUSE BASIN

Built in 1812 to serve inland waterway barges using the Regents Canal, it was enlarged in 1820 to accommodate seagoing vessels. The Basin also connects the Grand Union Canal to the Thames. Today it is the newest of London Docklands' four marinas and home to the Cruising Association. The Thames Path here links with the Lea Valley Walk via the Limehouse Cut.

25. THE GRAPES

Set amongst early 18th Century merchants' houses, this is almost certainly the same riverside pub as the one Dickens calls The Six Jolly Fellowship Porters in 'Our Mutual Friend'. While in Dickens' words 'the available space in it was not much larger than a hackney-coach', it has been extended sideways.

18. THE PROSPECT OF WHITBY

This famous pub was once the scene of bare knuckle and cock fighting. Turner, Whistler and other leading artists of their time sketched the Thames from here. There is a noon-dial anchor in the courtyard of Prospect Wharf, on which you can mark mid-day in both Greenwich Mean Time and British Summer Time.

19. SHADWELL BASIN

When ships outgrew the original London Docks in the 19th Century, Shadwell Basin was built in 1858 to provide the space they needed. The Basin today is used by a water sports centre, and provides an attractive setting for waterside housing. The red bascule bridges across the entrances date from the 1930s and have been preserved by the LDDC.

21. FREE TRADE WHARF

Originally built by the East India Company in 1795 for storing saltpetre, a main constituent of gunpowder. The entrance on The Highway is surmounted by the Company's coat of arms. Remodelled and added to, it was renamed Free Trade Wharf in 1858. Today, it is a very attractive mixed redevelopment.

22. LIMEHOUSE LINK

Completed in 1993, the 1.8 km Limehouse Link was the second largest civil engineering project in Europe after the Channel Tunnel. The sculpture over the entrance, Restless Dream, is one of three commissioned by the LDDC for the tunnel.

23. THE BARLEY MOW

Housed in the former Dockmaster's House at the entrance to Limehouse Basin, this waterside pub is named after an original 1730 Taylor Walker brewery on this site. This stretch of the Thames was known as Brewery Wharf and the original Barley Mow produced traditional ale that was shipped all over the world from the Wharf.

26. BOOTY'S

Opened as a wine bar in 1979, this was formerly a pub called The Waterman's Arms. Nearby is Duke's Shore (a corruption of 'sewer'), a small dock for barges awaiting repair.

27. THE HOUSE THEY LEFT BEHIND

Refurbished in 1986, the pub is all that remains of a terrace of buildings that stood on the site. Hops grew outside the pub, and you can still see some growing today. In the summer, you can play pétanque next to the Herring Gull, a steel and copper sculpture by Jane Ackroyd, commissioned by the LDDC.

28. ROPEMAKERS FIELDS

A new park created by the LDDC, and named after one of the area's important shipbuilding activities in the days of the docks - rope fibres needed a large open space to be first laid out so that they could then be twisted together. A copper roofed bandstand incorporating 19th Century warehouse columns is a feature of the park along with gate columns and railings with cast rope motifs.

Just over eight kilometres long, the Docklands section of the Thames Path stretches between Tower Bridge and the Greenwich Foot Tunnel. Closely following the Thames along some of the most interesting riverside in London, the path charts the fascinating and varied history of maritime London and Docklands.

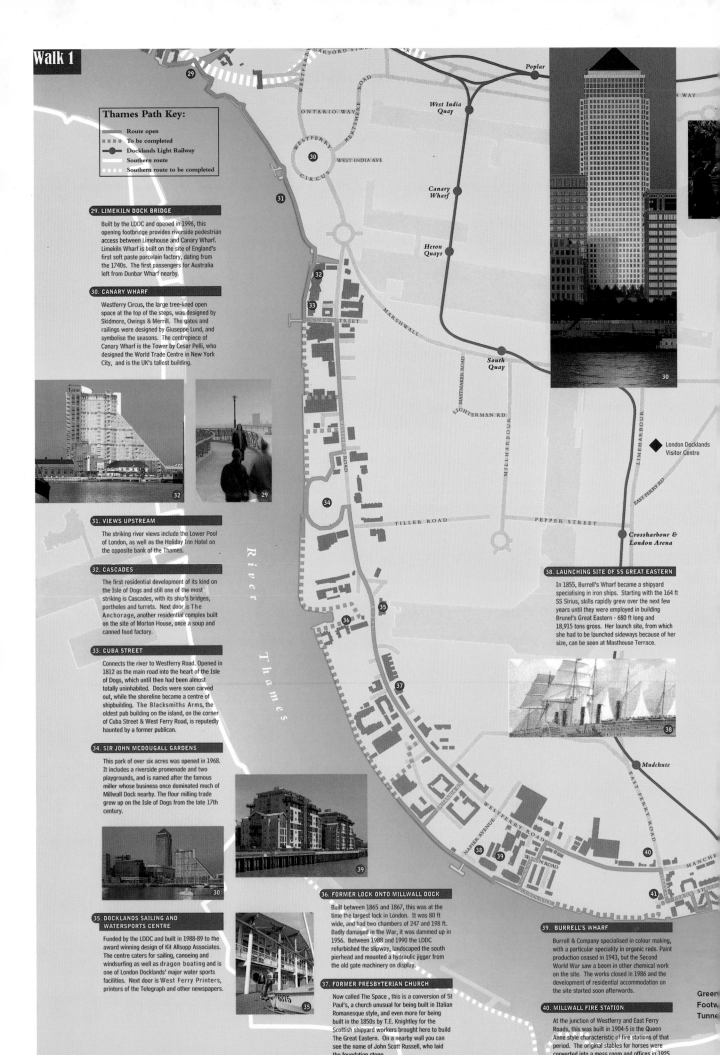

Thames Path Key:

- ━━━━ Route open
- ╍╍╍╍ To be completed
- ●━━●━━● Docklands Light Railway
- ━━━━ Southern route
- ╍╍╍╍ Southern route to be completed

29. LIMEKILN DOCK BRIDGE

Built by the LDDC and opened in 1996, this opening footbridge provides riverside pedestrian access between Limehouse and Canary Wharf. Limekiln Wharf is built on the site of England's first soft paste porcelain factory, dating from the 1740s. The first passengers for Australia left from Dunbar Wharf nearby.

30. CANARY WHARF

Westferry Circus, the large tree-lined open space at the top of the steps, was designed by Skidmore, Owings & Merrill. The gates and railings were designed by Giuseppe Lund, and symbolise the seasons. The centrepiece of Canary Wharf is the Tower by Cesar Pelli, who designed the World Trade Centre in New York City, and is the UK's tallest building.

31. VIEWS UPSTREAM

The striking river views include the Lower Pool of London, as well as the Holiday Inn Hotel on the opposite bank of the Thames.

32. CASCADES

The first residential development of its kind on the Isle of Dogs and still one of the most striking is Cascades, with its ship's bridges, portholes and turrets. Next door is The Anchorage, another residential complex built on the site of Morton House, once a soup and canned food factory.

33. CUBA STREET

Connects the river to Westferry Road. Opened in 1812 as the main road into the heart of the Isle of Dogs, which until then had been almost totally uninhabited. Docks were soon carved out, while the shoreline became a centre of shipbuilding. The Blacksmiths Arms, the oldest pub building on the island, on the corner of Cuba Street & West Ferry Road, is reputedly haunted by a former publican.

34. SIR JOHN MCDOUGALL GARDENS

This park of over six acres was opened in 1968. It includes a riverside promenade and two playgrounds, and is named after the famous miller whose business once dominated much of Millwall Dock nearby. The flour milling trade grew up on the Isle of Dogs from the late 17th century.

35. DOCKLANDS SAILING AND WATERSPORTS CENTRE

Funded by the LDDC and built in 1988-89 to the award winning design of Kit Allsopp Associates. The centre caters for sailing, canoeing and windsurfing as well as dragon boating and is one of London Docklands' major water sports facilities. Next door is West Ferry Printers, printers of the Telegraph and other newspapers.

36. FORMER LOCK ONTO MILLWALL DOCK

Built between 1865 and 1867, this was at the time the largest lock in London. It was 80 ft wide, and had two chambers of 247 and 198 ft. Badly damaged in the War, it was dammed up in 1956. Between 1988 and 1990 the LDDC refurbished the slipway, landscaped the south pierhead and mounted a hydraulic jigger from the old gate machinery on display.

37. FORMER PRESBYTERIAN CHURCH

Now called The Space , this is a conversion of St Paul's, a church unusual for being built in Italian Romanesque style, and even more for being built in the 1850s by T.E. Knightley for the Scottish shipyard workers brought here to build The Great Eastern. On a nearby wall you can see the name of John Scott Russell, who laid the foundation stone.

38. LAUNCHING SITE OF SS GREAT EASTERN

In 1855, Burrell's Wharf became a shipyard specialising in iron ships. Starting with the 164 ft SS Sirius, skills rapidly grew over the next few years until they were employed in building Brunel's Great Eastern - 680 ft long and 18,915 tons gross. Her launch site, from which she had to be launched sideways because of her size, can be seen at Masthouse Terrace.

39. BURRELL'S WHARF

Burrell & Company specialised in colour making, with a particular speciality in organic reds. Paint production ceased in 1943, but the Second World War saw a boom in other chemical work on the site. The works closed in 1986 and the development of residential accommodation on the site started soon afterwards.

40. MILLWALL FIRE STATION

At the junction of Westferry and East Ferry Roads, this was built in 1904-5 in the Queen Anne style characteristic of fire stations of that period. The original stables for horses were converted into a mess room and offices in 1925.

Map labels: Poplar · West India Quay · Canary Wharf · Heron Quays · South Quay · Crossharbour & London Arena · Mudchute · London Docklands Visitor Centre · WESTFERRY CIRCUS · WEST INDIA AVE · ONTARIO WAY · HERTSMERE ROAD · WESTFERRY ROAD · MARSHWALL · MASTMAKER ROAD · LIGHTERMAN RD · MILLHARBOUR · LIMEHARBOUR · EAST FERRY RD · TILLER ROAD · PEPPER STREET · NAPIER AVENUE · WESTFERRY ROAD · MANCHESTER · River Thames · Green Footw Tunne

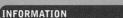

Preface

This book contains 27 guided walks illustrated with maps, engravings and photographs. They explore the colourful history of Central London and the development of Docklands from the glorious opening of the docks at the beginning of the 19th century to the dramatic regeneration over the last three decades of the second millennium. The walks can be enjoyed in any order, the numbering is only a kind of presentation. Happy walking.

Content

Internationally Acknowledged Books by Prof Naib

"London Millennium Guide" Ed., Ent., and Asp. ISBN 1 8745 36 201

"London Dockland Guide" Heritage Panorama ISBN 1 8745 36 031

"London Illustrated" History, Current & Future ISBN 1 8745 36 015

"Discover London Docklands" A to Z Guide ISBN 1 8745 36 007

"London Docklands" Past, Present and Future ISBN 1 8745 36 023

"European Docklands" Past, Present & Future ISBN 0 9019 87 824

"Dockland" Historical Survey ISBN 0 9089 87 800

"Fluid Mechanics, Hydraulics and Envir. Eng." ISBN 1 8745 36 066

"Applied Hydraulics, Hyd and Envir. Eng." ISBN 1 8745 36 058

"Jet Mechanics and Hydraulic Structures" ISBN 0 9019 87 832

"Experimental Fluid Mechs & Hyd Modelling" ISBN 1 8745 36 090

"Londons Water Heritage" 2000 years ISBN 18745 36 406

See information on the UEL web site
http://www.uel.ac.uk

The author is Professor of Civil Engineering and Head of Department at the University of East London, Longbridge Road, RM8 2AS, Great Britain.
(Tel: 020 8223 2478/2531, Fax: 020 8223 2963)

"London and Docklands Walks" ISBN 1874536 252

First Printing: July 2000

INFORMATION

How to get there

Docklands Light Railway runs a full daily service starting at Tower Gateway, Bank, Stratford, Beckton and Island Gardens. Westferry, Limehouse and Island Gardens are the closest stations to the Thames Path. Please ring 0171 363 9700 for more information.

For bus services ring the Travel Hotline on 0171 918 4000 (24 hour service).

Thames Path Information

For a free leaflet about the Thames Path contact :
Countryside Commission Postal Sales, PO Box 124, Walgrave, Northampton NN6 9TL. Telephone 01604 781848

An essential guide to anyone wanting to walk this national trail is 'The Thames Path' by David Sharp, published by Aurum Press.

41. FERRY STREET

The Ferry House pub once served the needs of people like Samuel Pepys crossing to and from Greenwich by ferry. At Midland Place you can walk down to a spectacular view across the river: the Cutty Sark is straight ahead, and Wren's Royal Naval Hospital is to the left.

42. JOHNSON'S DRAWDOCK

Much of the area to the north of Saunders Ness Road was occupied by industries which required access to the river. Access, however, was extremely limited and mainly provided by Johnson's Drawdock. Later used as a scrapyard, it was refurbished by the LDDC in 1988.

44. VIEW FROM ISLAND GARDENS

Dominating the view is the Queen's House designed by Inigo Jones to provide not merely a royal home for the wife of James I but also to link the palace with the park over the highway. Sir Christopher Wren was architect in charge of the new hospital for naval pensioners which subsequently became the Naval College in 1873. The Observatory was also designed by Wren. The Cutty Sark was launched as a china tea clipper in 1869 but enjoyed a more prosperous role in later years as a wool clipper.

45. THE GREENWICH FOOT TUNNEL

Built between 1900-02 by the London County Council the tunnel replaced the ferry service between the Isle of Dogs and Greenwich. It catered for the many people who lived on one side of the river and worked in the Docks on the other. It takes about 10 minutes to walk through including rides in the two lifts.

43. ISLAND GARDENS

This area was originally a dump and became known as 'Scrap Iron Park' in the early 19th Century. In the 1840s, the authorities at Greenwich Hospital across the river started to become seriously concerned at the pollution reaching them from industrial developments on the Isle of Dogs. However, it was not until 1895 that Island Gardens were laid out and opened to the public as a much needed riverside park space. This, the Naval authorities of the time noted, greatly improved the view from Greenwich. Today, it is the Canaletto style view across the Thames of Greenwich, the Royal Observatory and the Cutty Sark which makes Island Gardens so worth visiting.

Island Gardens entrance to the Greenwich Foot Tunnel

Greenwich Foot Tunnel links south bank and the north bank tes of the Thames Path.

North East Isle of Dogs

You can start this walk of about 5.5km from either South Quay or Crossharbour DLR station. The nearby Visitor Centre was closed in 1998. Alight at Crossharbour and turn left into Limeharbour. The impressive Harbour Exchange development is at the top of the road. Turn right along Marsh Wall, at the end of which is the Jack Dash community centre. Cross directly over Preston's Road where the footpath takes you to Stewart Street. Here you will find the Storm Water Pumping Station, built in 1988, and Pier Head Lock residential development (1). Return to Preston's Road and turn right, crossing the Dutch-style Blue Bridge (2), constructed by the Port of London Authority in 1969. Turn right into Coldharbour, a 19th century street of Captains' houses where the Gun Pub (3) is mainly of 19th century origin. Nelson House and Isle House (4) are fine examples, which can be found near the end of the street. They are privately owned. Leave Coldharbour and cross over to the other side of Preston's Road, head right and turn left into Bridge House Quay. Here you will find Bridge

House (5), a Georgian residence built in 1819 to house the Superintendent of the West India Dock Company. Now used as the offices of the London Federation of Boys Clubs. Return to Preston's Road, turn left and continue until you reach Aspen Way roundabout. On the way you see the restored East India Dock wall. On the east side of the roundabout you observe one of the last surviving hydraulic pumping stations in Docklands, built 1857. Follow the road round to the left until you reach Trafalgar Way. On the left there is a view of Blackwall Basin (6) and Poplar Dock (7), with its restored pair of cranes. In 1877, Poplar Western Dock was constructed to serve as the destination of colliers carrying coal to London. On the right you see the new Billingsgate Fish Market (8). At the end of Trafalgar Way turn right onto Churchill Place and cross the bridge. Here you have views of two new footbridges and many developments, including Heron Quays (9) and former West India Dock (10).

At the end of Churchill Place, turn right into

Canada Square containing the Tower, which is the Capital's most striking new building. Turn right into Adams Place and left along fisherman's Walk. Using the new pontoon bridge, cross the dock to the north side of West India Quay. Here you see Warehouses 1 & 2 (12). The Grade I listed buildings are the last surviving warehouses of their period. Go up the steps of Wren's Landing and continue through the tree-lined Cabot Square (13) and then left along South Colonnade. Turn right onto Nash Place and then right along Mackenzie Walk. Here the local pub provides waterside hospitality. Continue to the end and turn right until you reach West India Avenue, which leads to the beautiful Westferry Circus roundabout (14). Follow the roundabout on the left and go down the pedestrian walkway. At the bottom of the walkway continue forwards and cross the bridge over the City Canal (15) and onto Marsh Wall. Proceed to the elevated South Quay DLR station. From here you can see South Quay Plazza (16) and the Thames Quay (17) as well as Millwall Inner Dock.

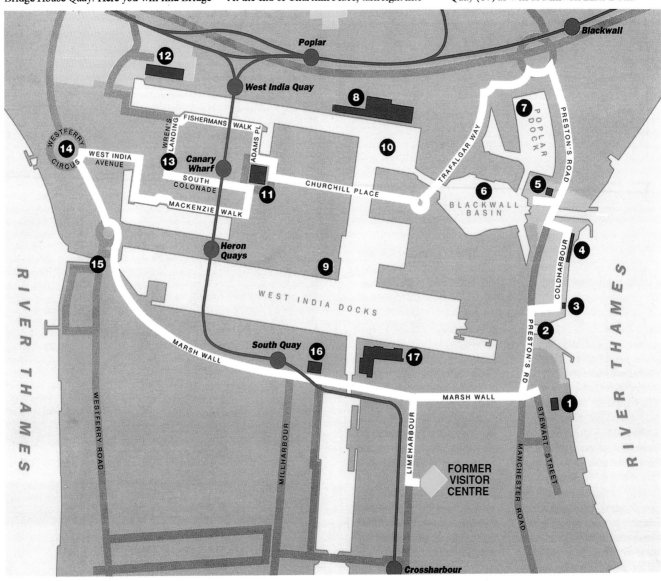

DLR Crossharbour Station close to the London Arena.

Junction of Limeharbour with Marsh Wall showing new office developments.

Jack Dash Community Centre in Marsh Wall.

Pier Head Lock (1), luxury apartments next to the Blue Bridge (2) and overlooking the Thames and the Millennium Dome.

The Gun Pub.

19th century Isle House (4) adjoining Nelson House.

The Bridge House (5), built in 1819 to house the Superintendent of the West India Dock Company.

Renovated railway crane at Poplar Docks (7).

New Billingsgate Fish Market (8) built 1982 on North Quay.

The Grade I listed Sugar Warehouses I and II (12), on the North Quay, housing Museum on Docklands and luxury apartments.

North Quay warehouses overlooking the old West India Import Dock, c1830.

South East Isle of Dogs

From Crossharbour DLR Station enter into Limeharbour and turn right, then left into the entrance of Asda's Superstore (1), one of two built in Docklands during the 1980s, the other being at Beckton. Continue to the bottom of the car park. Turn right and follow a pathway at the corner of the car park. Pass through a gateway and continue along the path and you find yourself in the 13-hectare Mudchute City Farm (2). Stay on the track until you reach Pier Street, at the end of which you will find yourself on Manchester Road. Cross the road and then turn on to Chichester Way. Continue along here and you will reach the start of a river walkway. On the left you can see London Yard (3), a Dutch-style development of flats and houses with views of Blackwall and the Millennium Dome across the river. Turn right along the river walkway. The flats on your right are part of the Compass Point (4) complex which contains a wide variety of architectural styles. Opposite the memorial to the victims of a 1969 industrial accident, turn right in to

Sextant Avenue. Take a left along Saunders Ness Road and left along Storers Quay to re-join the river walkway.

Continue along the walkway until you reach Newcastle Drawdock (5) where barges used to unload at low tide. Just past the end of the drawdock on Glenaffric Avenue is the Church of Christ and St.John (6). On the other side of the drawdock the riverside walkway continues past Cumberland Mills estate (7) which features four pyramids and roof top gardens with magnificent views of the river and Greenwich. Continue and you will enter Island Gardens (8). From here you have one of the finest views in London. Across the river is Greenwich University and the Royal Naval College (9) designed by Sir Christopher Wren in 1695. A foot tunnel, opened in 1902, runs below the Thames from Island Gardens to Greenwich. Further to the east turn left on to Ferry Street where you will find the Ferry House pub (10), an early 19th century building

with a tower for keeping watch for the old Greenwich Ferry. It is recorded that Pepys used this ferry in 1665.

Turn right and cross Manchester Road and continue up East Ferry Road. The new Island Gardens station can be seen nearby. On the right you will find Millwall Railway Viaduct (11) which was built in 1872 and is currently used by the Docklands Light Railway. Continue through the attractive Chapel House Estate (12) until you see, on the left, a large red brick chimney. Almost immediately after the chimney on the east side of Millwall Outer Dock, turn left and down some steps under the DLR line and into Millwall Dock (13). Turn right and continue along the walkway with an excellent view of Greenwich View office development (14). When you reach Turnberry Street turn right on to Pepper Street and then left on to Limeharbour and return to Crossharbour Station. The nearby Visitor Centre closed in 1998. The walk is 4.7km.

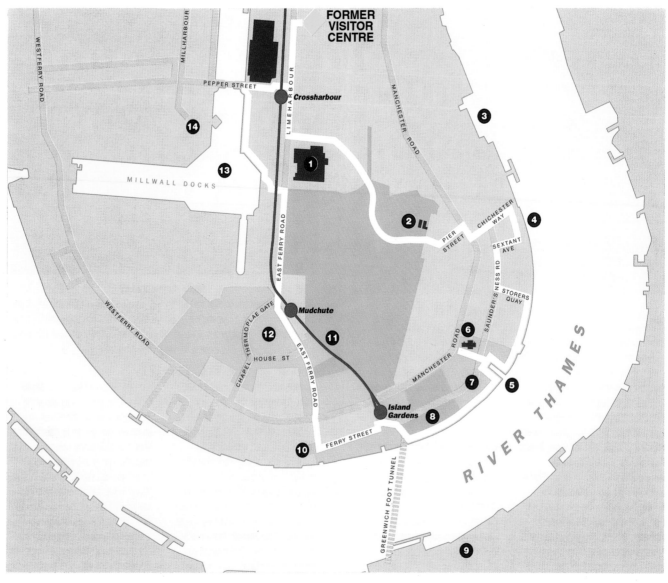

Cottage-style housing on the Chapel House Estate (12) conservation area.

The Manchester Road Post Office, c1982.

Right: Mudchute Farm (2), largest London city farm with riding school, formed from mud dredged from the Millwall Dock.

Compass Point (4), the 100-homes complex with gabled façades and bow-fronted bays.

London Yard (3), a Dutch-style development with a river beach.

Cumberland Mills (7) and Newcastle Draw Dock (5).

Millwall Viaduct (11), built 1872, used by the Docklands Light Railway.

Riverside Island Gardens (8) laid in the 19th century.

Victorian Church of Christ & St John (6), c1880.

Bird watching and ornithology board alongside Millwall Dock.

The magnificent Royal Naval College and the Queen's House at Greenwich (9) from Island Gardens, one of the finest views in London.

North West Isle of Dogs

From DLR Crossharbour station turn left along Limeharbour onto Pepper Street. Cross the bridge that spans Millwall Dock through Glengall Bridge (1), a new development of houses, shops and offices completed in 1989. In 1963 the Port of London Authority built a covered bridge with glass sides to provide public access across Millwall Dock. At the end of Pepper Street, cross Millharbour and through the entrance to Tiller Road, turn right and then left on to Mellish Street.

Continue until the end of the street, cross the road and then right along Westferry Road. Carry on until you reach the Blacksmith's Arms pub (2) on your right. This pub was built in the early 19th century and is reputed to be haunted by the ghost of a former landlord. Turn left on to Cuba Street, which is opposite the pub, and then right along a river walkway. Pass The Anchorage (3), a large residential complex built on the site of the old Morton House, the soup and canned food factory. The adjoining building is known as Cascades (4) with its unique cascading silhouette dominating the river frontage to the Isle of Dogs. Facing this building is the City Pride pub. Turn right at the end of Cascades and rejoin Marsh Wall. Continue along the walkway to Westferry Circus and follow the roundabout on the left.

Go down the steps at the end of the walkway and continue along Westferry Road and then turn right into Garford Street. On the right are the Dock Police Cottages (5), built in 1819 to house the police staff employed within the Dock Estate. Slightly further on is the elegant Salvation Army Hostel (6), of Queen Anne style. At the end of Garford Street, turn right and then right again on to Hertsmere Road. On the right hand side of the road stands the Georgian Dockmaster's House (7), which is now a restaurant. Where the road splits you see the Ledger Building (8) and adjacent are the magnificent early 19th century Warehouses 1 and 2 (9). Take the right hand road with the Cannon Workshops (10) on your right. Nearby is the Round Guard House used in the old days for armoury and temporary lock-up for thieves. When you reach the Barclays Bank building, climb the steps and walk along the right-hand side of the building and follow the small walkway on the right that leads to Fisherman's Walk and turn right on to Adams Place and then left on to Canada Square, home of the spectacular tower called No.1 Canada Square (11). Carry on round the Square and continue along South Colonnade and then down Cubitt Steps on the left. Turn right, continue to the end of Mackenzie Walk until you reach West India Avenue. Turn left and you will arrive at Westferry Circus roundabout. Follow the roundabout on the left and go down the pedestrian walkway. At the bottom of the walkway continue forwards, past the roundabout and cross the bridge over the City Canal (12), past the 1909 pumping station and on to Marsh Wall. Cross the road at South Quay Plaza (13) and follow the walkway on the left that runs along Millwall Dock (14) with a magnificent view of Harbour Exchange buildings (15). When you reach Pepper Street turn left and cross Glengall Bridge. At Limeharbour turn right and return to the Crossharbour station.

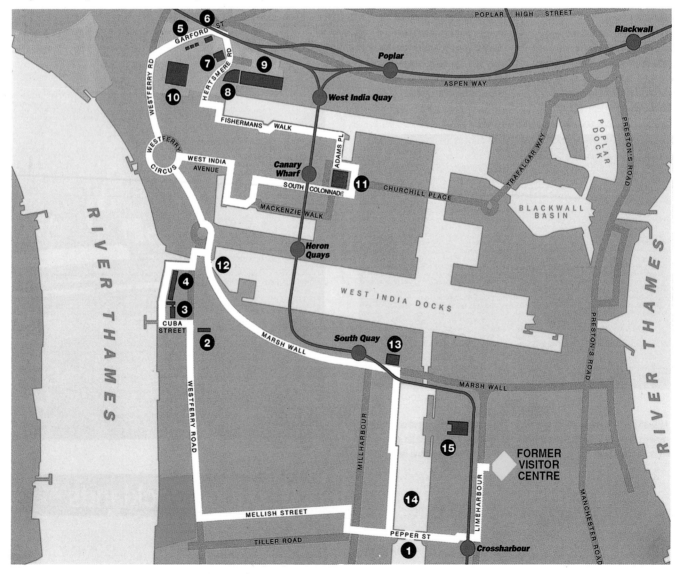

Top: Glengall Bridge (1), a mixed development with a lifting bridge across Millwall Dock (14). Right: Harbour Exchange office blocks (15), c1990.

An impressive view across Millwall Dock from Glengall Bridge of South Quay Plaza and Canary Wharf, c1996.

Housing developments of Anchorage (3) and Cascades (4) from the south.

Ledger Building (8) formerly the General Office for the Port of London where records of cargoes were kept.

Early 19th century engraving of the West India Import Dock, showing the sugar warehouses on the north quay.

The magnificent listed Grade I Sugar Warehouses (9) and the dockside sheds (now demolished) circa 1982.

The former Port of London Cannon Workshops (10) have now been converted into small business units.

Lord Admiral met with workers in West India Graving Dock previously adjacent to Blackwall Basin, c1941.

A bustling scene at the North Quay seen from south-east, c1830.

Cabot Square and Canada Square (11) with Canary Wharf Tower, complemented by watercourts.

The beautiful Westferry Circus, overlooking the River Thames and Canary Wharf Pier.

View from City Canal Lock of South West India Dock, with every berth occupied by boats, c1934.

View from Blue Bridge of developments along the South Quay, c1992.

South Quay Footbridge. Heron Quays roundabout sculpture.
Left: Aerial view of Canary Wharf and North West Isle of Dogs.

An aerial view looking towards the city of the north west corner of the Isle of Dogs, c1995.

The renovated and converted Sugar Warehouse connected by a pontoon footbridge to Canary Wharf, c1998.

Dock workers sifting sugar into sacks in the North Quay warehouses, c1930.

Interior of the newly converted apartments in the North Quay warehouses, c1999.

Busy activities along the North Quay with carts waiting to be loaded with casks, late 19th century.

Artist impression of the Museum in Docklands inside the sugar warehouses.

Sugar sacks drying along the North Quay and dock workers moving sugar bags from the sheds into warehouses, c1938.

City Pride pub near the entrance of the former City Canal (12).

The waterside restaurant at the entrance to Millwall Dock, a short distance from South Quay Plaza (13).

This walk about 4.6km, starts at Crossharbour DLR station. Turn left into Pepper Street and cross the bridge spanning Millwall Dock and through Glengall Bridge (1), newly developed apartments, shops and offices completed in 1989. At the end of Pepper Street follow the map into Westferry Road.

Continue along Westferry Road until you reach the former St Paul's Presbyterian Church (2), now converted into the Space Arts Centre for Music with relaxed surroundings. Cross the road and turn in to Claude Street and then left into Homer Drive and Cyclops Wharf (3), riverside flats and mews houses. Turn left through Cyclops Mews and back on to Westferry Road. Turn right and carry on and turn right at Napier Avenue. Running alongside you will find the shipyard of Burrell's Wharf (4), where the Great Eastern ship was built. Turn left on to Blasker Walk, turn left again to enter Burrell's Wharf Square (5). Return to Blasker Walk and turn left on to Rainbow Avenue. Cross Wynan Road and immediately on the right is Maconochies Road, the country's largest self-built development. Carry on along this road, cross over Westferry Road and along Chapel House Street which runs through the attractive Chapel House Estate (6).

When the road splits in two turn left on to Thermopylae Gate. At the end cross over the road and turn left along East Ferry Road. You will come to an old brick chimney on the left, turn left here and go down the steps which take you under the DLR line and into Millwall Dock (7), where you find Clipper Quay housing surrounding the former Graving Dock. Turn right and continue along the walkway giving an excellent view of the new office development of Greenwich View (8). When you reach Turnberry Street turn right on to Pepper Street and return to Crossharbour Station.

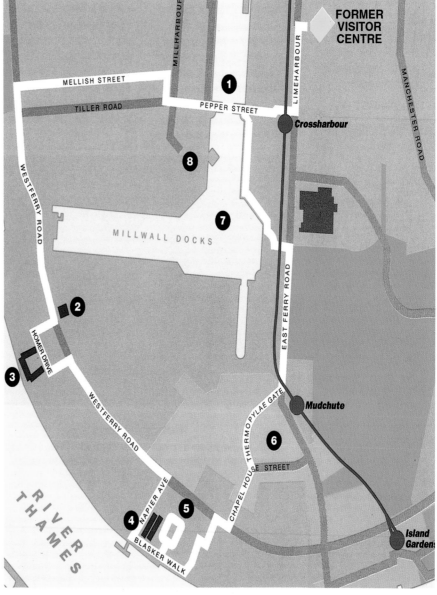

Brunel's masterpiece the Great Eastern ship built 1853-58.

Cyclops Wharf (3) homes.   Sailing Centre, Millwall.

Left:Hogarth's engraving showing a gibbet, c1750.

The Daily Telegraph automated printing works on the north side of Millwall Dock.

Construction of Brunel's Great Eastern ship at Burrells Wharf (4), c1858.

The tea clipper Cutty Sark at Greenwich.

Greenwich View office development (8), west of Millwall Dock.

The derelict Burrell's Wharf and Brunel's ship launch site, c1982, now luxury new homes with conservation features, c1998.

The old granary (demolished) and busy dockside loading, c1950s, at Millwall Dock, site of Greenwich View (8).

The Space Art Centre (2), a converted church providing programmes for the local community.

Clipper Quay waterside homes at the former Millwall Dry Dock (7).

Poplar and Blackwall

A convenient point to start this trail of about 2.5km is DLR Westferry Station. Walk a short distance along Westferry Road and take the first left into Garford Street. On the right you can see three Georgian Dock Police cottages (1), built 1819. Further along is the Salvation Army Building (2). Cross West India Dock Road into Ming Street leading to Poplar High Street. Near the junction of Woodstock Terrace and the High Street is the former East India Dock Company's Chaplain's House (3), and next to that is the charming former Poplar Town Hall (4), now a housing office. Along Woodstock Terrace you find attractive 19th century houses facing the historic St Matthias Church (5), the oldest building in Docklands. Visits can be arranged by appointment.

Return to Poplar High Street, turn left and proceed to Robin Hood Lane. On the other side of Blackwall Tunnel Approach you find the headquarters of the Financial Times (6). The large printing works can be seen through the 93m glass wall. Adjacent to it is the impressive East India complex of offices surrounding the old East India Export Dock. Return to Woolmore Street, cross over Cotton Street and follow a path to Bazely Street. Here you find the historic All Saints Church, built around 1820, its splendid rectory and a large garden with mature trees.

Walk back to Poplar High Street and continue along it until you reach Naval Row. On the

south side of this narrow road is the Steamship Pub and on the north side is the original East India Import Dock Wall, c1806. Further east is the listed hydraulic pumping station. Find your way to the elevated DLR station of Blackwall for your next destination. The red brick building of Brunswick Wharf is clearly visible. It was built in 1956 as a power station on part of the site of the old East India Export Dock.

If you wish to explore Blackwall further, proceed along Aspen Way until you reach the roundabout where you see the remains of the original East India Dock Wall, c1806. Take the

second exit off the roundabout to the road bridge and on your right is the confluence of the River Lee with the Thames with a number of wildlife developments. The Limmo site on the last loop of Bow Creek is a £3.5m scheme which has created a park, adjacent to the old East India Dock Basin, for visitors and children to enjoy and learn. Also near the park is Trinity Buoy Wharf and Lighthouse, which was the centre of Trinity House, the company responsible for the operation of all lighthouses around the UK coastline for 185 years. The beautiful octagonal lighthouse, built around 1860, is unique and the complex has recently been converted into an arts centre.

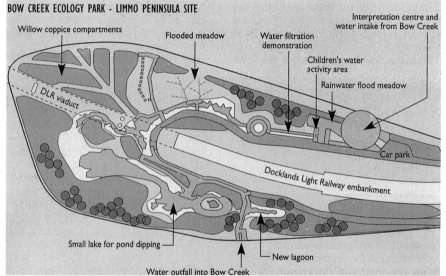

BOW CREEK ECOLOGY PARK - LIMMO PENINSULA SITE

Willow coppice compartments · Flooded meadow · Water filtration demonstration · Interpretation centre and water intake from Bow Creek · Children's water activity area · Rainwater flood meadow · DLR viaduct · Car park · Docklands Light Railway embankment · Small lake for pond dipping · New lagoon · Water outfall into Bow Creek

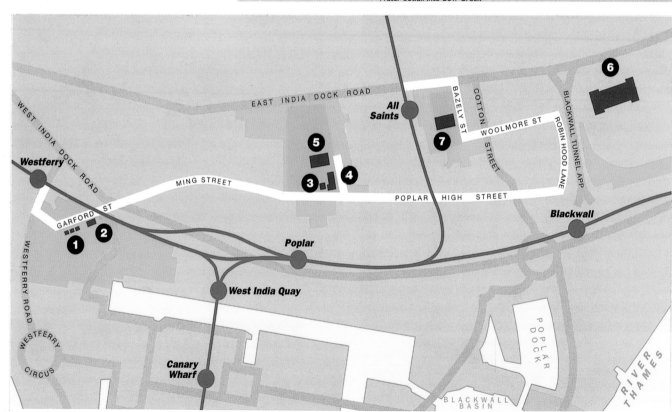

Dock Police Cottages (1) in Garford Street, now privately owned, c1819.

The Dock Masters House, c1807, near the Salvation Army Hostel (2), now a restaurant.

St Matthias Old Church (5), oldest building in London Docklands, built for East India Dock Company, c1654.

The former Victorian Poplar Town Hall (4) in the High Street is Grade II listed.

Top: Financial Times Printing Works (6), fronting East India Dock Road. Right: All Saints Church (7) with Portland Stone facade, c1820.

Top: Perrys Dock and Masthouse at Blackwell, c1801. Bottom: The East India Import and Export Docks built on the site of Perrys Dock, c1806.

East India Dock office complex adjacent to the Financial Times, built on the south west part of the former East India Docks.

This walk starts around the Tower of London and covers the Thames Path at Wapping. It is about 5.8km long. From either Tower Hill tube station or Tower Gateway DLR station make your way to the left-hand side of Tower Bridge. Go down the steps and pass Commodity quay into St.Katherine Docks. Carry on along the covered walkway and turn right into Ivory House (1). Go through Ivory House and turn right. Cross the drawbridge and turn left and cross another drawbridge where you find the 19th century Dockmaster's House and Swing Bridge (2). Keep to the left and follow the cobbled pathway until you reach Marble Quay and you see Dickens Inn (3) and Telford Bridge (4). Turn left on to Mews Street and follow round to the left. At the end of Mews Street turn right along Thomas More Street, cross over and take the riverside walkway that starts almost opposite St.Katherine's Way. This takes you back on to St. Katherine's Way, turn right and continue along Wapping High Street and into the Wapping Pierhead Conservation Area. On the right are the attractive Wapping Pierhead Houses (5) built between 1811-13 with the Town of Ramsgate pub (6) adjacent to them. As you turn left into Scandrett Street in order to see St. John's Church (7) built in 1756

And bombed during the Second World War, only the distinctive tower remains.

Return to Wapping High Street and continue along until you reach Oliver's Wharf (8) which was built circa 1870 and was the first to be converted into flats in Docklands. After that there is St.John's Wharf (9) and the Captain Kidd pub (10), so named because it is close to Execution Dock where many pirates, including Captain Kidd, were executed. King Henry's Wharf (11) and the converted Gun Wharves (12) are both Grade 2 listed buildings and are fine examples of Victorian warehouse architecture. Just after Wapping underground station and opposite Clave Street is a gate leading to a riverside walkway. Along this walkway you see on your left the residential developments of Towerside and St. Hilda's Wharf (13). Follow the walkway until it returns to Wapping High Street and you see on your right New Crane Wharf (14), one of the loveliest warehouse developments in Docklands. Continue past the Grade I listed New Crane Wharf and turn right on to Wapping Wall. This street has several more warehouse conversions, including Metropolitan Wharf (15), a centre for small businesses.

Further on is The Prospect of Whitby pub (16). There has been a pub here since the 16th century and Samuel Pepys and Charles Dickens both drank here. Opposite you can see the now derelict London Hydraulic Pumping Station (17). The red brick Grade 2 listed building with a fine accumulator tower has been a landmark for over a century. Take the riverside walkway at the left of the pub and follow it until it ends at Glamis Road. Cross the road and turn right. Continue for a little way and then turn left into the new residential development of Shadwell Basin. The Basin is the only surviving part of London Docks and is used as a water sport training centre for young people. Turn left and follow the path around the Basin. On your right and up a small flight of stairs is St. Paul's Church, built 1821 and it includes a row of early 19th century cottages facing the graveyard (18). Continue around until you reach the start of the Wapping Wood Canal. Follow the path next to the canal past Tobacco Dock shopping centre (19), until you reach Thomas More Street. Turn left into Mews Street and right at the start of the marina. Follow the path around to the left then turn right just before Commodity Quay on to East Smithfield. Turn left and return to Tower Bridge.

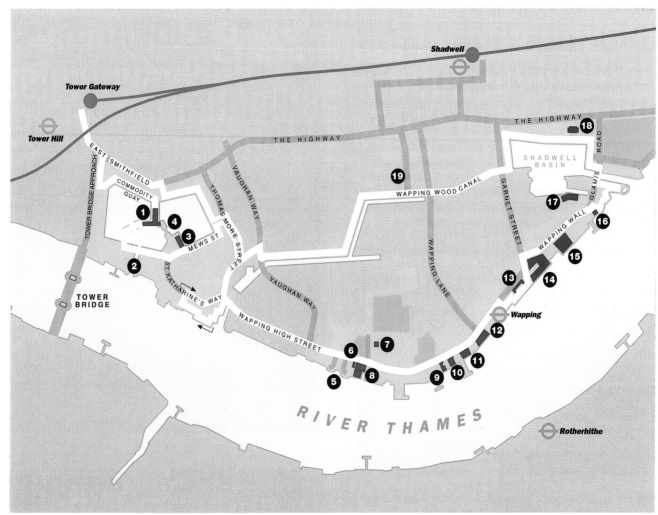

Aerial photograph showing St Katharines Docks adjacent to Tower of London and Tower Bridge. Ivory House is at the centre of the picture, c 1996.

Opening of St Katharines Docks with the arrival of the first ship from the West Indies, c 1828.

A view of Dickens Inn, Ivory House (1) and visiting historical ships in St Katharines Docks, c1980s.

Dickens Inn pub (3), converted from a warehouse, and new Telford Bridge (4), c 1998.

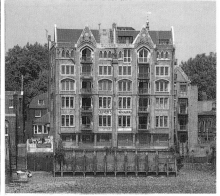

Wapping High Street with the entrance to the Town of Ramsgate pub shown near the centre.

Left: Wapping Pier Housing (5) built 1814, now converted into luxury apartments.

Oliver's Wharf (8), built c1870 was the first to be converted into flats in Docklands, with the Town of Ramsgate Pub at its side.

River view of Wapping converted warehouses, Police Station, St Johns Wharf (9) and Captain Kidd's public house (10).

Gun Wharves (12), Grade II listed Victorian warehouses converted into luxury riverside apartments, c1980s.

The converted riverside Metropolitan Wharf.

Tower of St John's church, c1756.

Hydraulic Pumping Station at Shadwell Basin (17), c1880s.

The magnificent King Henry Wharf (11), Grade II listed Victorian warehouses.

The converted Grade I listed New Crane Wharf (14) at Wapping Wall overlooking the River Thames.

The famous Prospect of Whitby pub (16), believed to be the oldest in London, c1980s.

King Edward VII memorial park adjacent to Shadwell Basin.

Right: Aerial view of Thames riverside from Shadwell to Canary Wharf, c1998. Top: Towerside and St Hilda's Wharf (13).

North Wapping & Limehouse

This walk, about 4km long, starts at Shadwell Station and ends at Westferry DLR station near Canary Wharf. From either Shadwell tube or DLR station turn right along Cable Street. On the left you will see St George's Town Hall (1) which has a striking mural depicting the fight between local residents and the British Union of Fascists in 1936. At the end of Cable Street turn left on to Cannon Street Road. Near the end of the road is the Church of St George in the East (2), an English Baroque architectural masterpiece by Nicholas Hawksmoor early 18th century.

Cross to the other side of The Highway and enter Tobacco Dock (3), a magnificent 19th century Grade 1 listed building converted into a shopping centre in 1989. Go to the end of Tobacco Dock where two replica ships are housed along the quayside. They are typical examples of the type which traded in the London Docks early 1800. At Wapping Wood Canal turn left along the canal walkway. Here the docks have been filled and the reclaimed Western Dock developed into canal-side housing. Carry on along the main path and you reach the new residential development of Shadwell Basin. The Basin was built in 1858 as part of the London Docks. Turn left and follow the Basin. On the left and up a small flight of stairs is St. Paul's Church (4), circa 1821. At the main entrance to Shadwell Basin cross over

Glamis Road lifting bridge and turn left and then right along Shadwell Dock Place. At the bottom turn left along the riverside walkway, which offers excellent views of Rotherhithe and Bermondsey.

Turn left into Free Trade Wharf (5) which was built in 1793 by the East India Dock Company, and then right along the Highway. Carry on into Narrow Street. Many of the former Captain houses on this street date from the mid 18th century. The street provided a setting for several of Charles Dickens' books, most especially 'Dombey and Son'. It is here where the Limehouse Link Tunnel starts. At the entrance to Limehouse Basin is the Barley Mow pub (6) which is a conversion of a 19th century Dockmaster's house. Further along Narrow Street is The Grapes pub (7) which Dickens used in 'Our Mutual Friend' renaming it 'The Six Jolly Fellowship Porters'. Limehouse Basin has been completely redeveloped into a major marina for Londoners. From The Grapes cross over diagonally to the right on to Ropemakers' Fields with the curiously-named The House They Left Behind pub (8). (Left behind after demolition of adjacent buildings).

Go through the park entrance on the right of the pub and turn left along the walkway. When the walkway splits into three, turn right and this

will lead to a walkway alongside Limehouse Cut Canal called Maize Row. There is a small passage on the right which will take you to Newell Street and St. Anne's Passage and Church (9) directly in front of you. Turn right along Newell Street and follow it to the end. Turn right down Three Colt Street and cross over Limehouse Causeway and continue down Emmet Street. On your right is Limekiln Dock (10), a 19th century warehouse converted to homes and shops. There is a new swing footbridge across the entrance to the dock as part of Thames Path. Return to Limehouse Causeway and turn right until you reach Westferry DLR station. You are a stone's throw from Canary Wharf.

DICKENS.

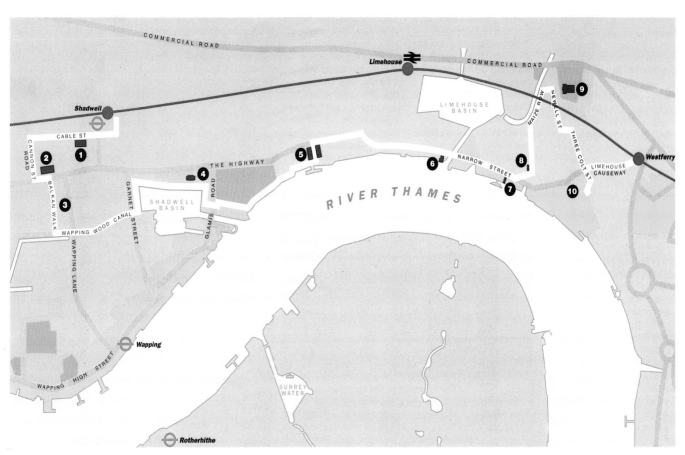

19

Church of St George in the East (2), c1729.

The entrance to the converted Tobacco Dock shopping precinct (3), c1990.

The entrance (top) of Tobacco Dock from the London dock c1890s.

Weighing and sampling at the Great Tobacco Warehouse at London Docks, c1856.

A replica of an 18th century sailing ship at Tobacco Dock.

Aerial view of Wapping in 1961, showing St Katharine Docks, London Docks and Shadwell Basin.

The attractive path for walkers along Wapping Canal.

The vaults at Tobacco Dock converted into malls with small shops, c1988.

The old and new Free Trade Wharf (5) with a restored Thames sailing barge.

Converted Sun Wharf in Narrow Street.

Top: New Housing development overlooking Shadwell Basin, c1998.

Left: St Pauls Church (4), built 1821, with steps leading to Shadwell Basin.

Top: The new marina and leisure centre in Limehouse Basin surrounded by new housing, c1998.

Left: The Grapes Pub (7), and former 18th century Captains Houses in Narrow Street.

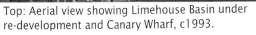

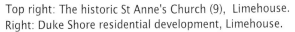

Top: Aerial view showing Limehouse Basin under re-development and Canary Wharf, c1993.

Top right: The historic St Anne's Church (9), Limehouse.
Right: Duke Shore residential development, Limehouse.

Surrey Quays & Rotherhithe

Nearly 7km long, this trail follows the old maritime district of Rotherhithe and the former Surrey Docks. Both Rotherhithe and Canada Water tube stations are convenient starting points. Starting at Rotherhithe underground station, turn left out of the entrance and then almost immediately left on to Railway Avenue and then left again into Tunnel Road. Here you have entered St Mary's Church Conservation Area. The first building you will see is the Brunel Engine House (1). This was built in 1842 and formerly housed the steam driven pumps to drain water during the construction of the Thames Tunnel. Turn right just after the Engine House and when you reach Rotherhithe Street it is worth making a small detour to the left to see St. Mary's Church (2) which was built in 1715 on the remains of an older one of Saxon times.

On returning to the start of Tunnel Road the early nineteenth century Thames Tunnel Mills (3) is opposite. This is a fine residential accommodation. Next door is the famous 17th

century Mayflower pub (4). In 1620 the sailing ship Mayflower moored here before her departure to Plymouth and then to America with the Pilgrim Fathers. Continue up Rotherhithe Street and pass a small garden with large rope sculptures set into cobblestones. Turn left just after the garden and walk along the riverside walkway which offers fine views of Wapping. On your right is the residential development Isambard Place (5).

Carry on until you return to Rotherhithe Street, turn right and continue. Look out for Bylands Close on the right-hand side of the road. Opposite you will find riverside residential development King and Queen Wharf (6). On the left of the Wharf go along the walkway that leads to the river and follow the walkway until it returns to Rotherhithe Street. Turn left and pass Globe Wharf (7), a rice warehouse until 1983. Just before the next bridge turn right into Lavender Pond and Pump House (8) which is a centre for a nature reserve. It was built by the Port of London Authority in 1928.

Turn right on returning to Rotherhithe Street until you come to the entrance to Heron Place. A short flight of stairs will take you to Acorn Walk (9), a 1930s housing estate with Art Deco exteriors. Directly opposite the rear exit gate is Nelson House (10), dating back to 1740 and now part of the Holiday Inn. Just as you leave Acorn Walk there is a pathway on the right called Nelson Walk. Take this pathway, turning right when the pathway splits. When the pathway splits again turn left on to Waterman's Walk. You are now in Stave Hill Ecological Park (11) which has two lakes and woodland. From the top of man-made Stave Hill you have excellent views of the City and Docklands. Follow the main pathway until you reach Redriff Road. Cross the road and continue on Onega Gate, which is almost directly opposite Waterman's Walk. Carry on until you reach the magnificent Greenland Dock (12), which during the 18th century was used by the Greenland Whaling Company. Later the dock became the main centre in the UK for the import of Scandinavian timber.

Continue left and then right on to South Sea Street. On your left are the listed Greenland Bridge and Lock (13), both dating from the nineteenth century. Turn right and follow the dock until you reach the start of Brunswick Quay. Climb the steps on the left of Brunswick Quay, cross Redriff Road and turn right and left on to Surrey Quays Road. On the right is Associated News Works (14), the printing works for the Mails newspapers and the Evening Standard. Pass the Surrey Quays Retail Centre on the left, where you can rest and have refreshments. Turn left and then right along Canada Water (15) until you re-join Surrey Quays Road. On the left is the old Dock Manager's Offices (16) which were completed in 1887. At the end of the road turn right on to Lower Road. Turn right when you reach the roundabout and you will find St Olave's Church (17), opened in 1927 for Norwegian seamen it still serves as the church for London's Norwegian community. Cross over the road that leads to the Rotherhithe Tunnel and turn right on to Brunel Road which will lead you back to Rotherhithe underground station.

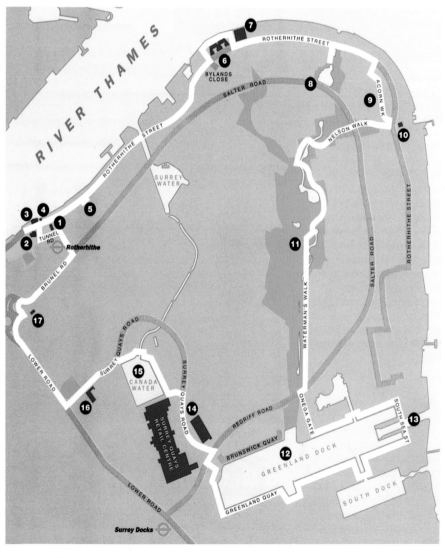

Thames Tunnel Mills apartments (3) and St Mary's Church (2), c1715.

Holiday Inn Hotel incorporating Columbia Wharf near Acorn Walk.

Tesco shopping precinct next to Canada Water (15).

Acorn Walk (9) built for dockers, c1930.

Top: Walks and cycle tracks along the Surrey Canal.
Left: Stave Hill (11) with views of City and Docklands.

Historic Nelson House (10), dating back to 1740.

Top: Surrey Docks City Farm, near Greenland Dock, with a variety of animals and a valuable education centre. Right: Life-size sculptures of sheep and goats fronting the City Farm along the Thames Path.
Left: Views of Greenland Dock (12) with residential estates and sailing facilities.

The old Greenland Entrance Bridge (13) with original features.

The former Surrey Docks Manager's Office (16), c1887.

Globe Wharf (7), a rice warehouse until 1983.

St Olaves Church (17), opened 1927.

Bermondsey & South Bank

You may start this walk of 3.7km either at Rotherhithe, Canada Water or Bermondsey tube station. Starting at Rotherhithe station, turn left out of the entrance into Railway Avenue and then left again into Tunnel Road. Here you have entered St Mary's Church Conservation Area. The first building you will see is the Brunel Engine House (1). Opposite the end of Tunnel Road is the famous 17th century Mayflower pub (2) and adjacent to it are the early nineteenth century Thames Tunnel Mills converted warehouses (3). Turn left and on the left is St. Mary's Church (4) which was built in 1715. Carry on along this walkway and on to Bermondsey Wall East until you reach the beautiful riverside Angel Pub (5) which is nearly 400 years old. In the 18th century it became the haunt of smugglers and famous personalities like Captain Cook. Opposite the Angel are the new housing developments of Cherry Garden Pier and the remains of Edward III's Manor House (6) which dates back to the 14th century. Take the riverside walkway after the Angel Pub which will return you to Bermondsey Wall East. Carry on along this road, turn left on to Loftie Street and then right along Chambers Street. Turn right on to George Row and then left on to Bermondsey Wall West.

Turning left you can see on your right Jacob's Island (7), now a residential and commercial development but once known as Folly Ditch, described by Charles Dickens in 'Oliver Twist'.

Adjacent to this is the distinctive China Wharf (8). You can now either use the footbridge to cross St Saviour Dock into Butlers Wharf or turn left on Mill Street and on your right are New Concordia Wharf and Vogan Mill (9) both magnificent nineteenth century warehouses converted into apartments. At the bottom of Mill Street turn right on to Tooley Street and then right again on to Shad Thames. Shad Thames, with its tall buildings connected by a criss-cross of bridges is one of the most distinctive Victorian streets in London. On the right are Christians and Java Wharves (10), Victorian tea and spice warehouses converted in 1988 into luxury penthouses. When Shad Thames bends to the left you will see the Design Museum (11), opened in 1989 by the Conran Foundation. Continue along Shad Thames with Butlers Wharf(12), built between 1871-3, on your right. Next to that is the Victorian Anchor Brewhouse (13). Continue until you arrive at Tower Bridge (14).

Cross over the road and continue along the riverside walkway. The headquarters of the Mayor of London and the Greater London Authority are being built here overlooking the Thames. Moored on the Thames is HMS Belfast (15). Built in 1938 she saw active service in the Second World War and is now a museum of naval history. Further along on the left is Hay's Galleria (16), a beautiful shopping precinct with restaurants and the Horniman riverside pub.

Opposite London Bridge City Pier is the new office development Cotton's Building (17). This is followed by London Bridge Hospital (18), which retains the façade of a Grade 2 listed Victorian warehouse, then St Olaf's House (19), built in 1931 and one of the finest examples of Art Deco architecture in Britain. At the end of the walkway go up the steps to London Bridge (20), cross the road and step down into the grounds of Southwark Cathedral. Walk on to Clink Street where you may see a replica of the Golden Hind which was used by Sir Francis Drake and further along is the Clink Prison Museum. Past Clink Street is the New Globe Theatre, where Shakespeare's plays are performed. Adjacent to the Globe is the old Bankside Power Station beautifully converted into the New Tate Gallery to house the modern collection of Matisse, Glocometti, Henry Moore and others.

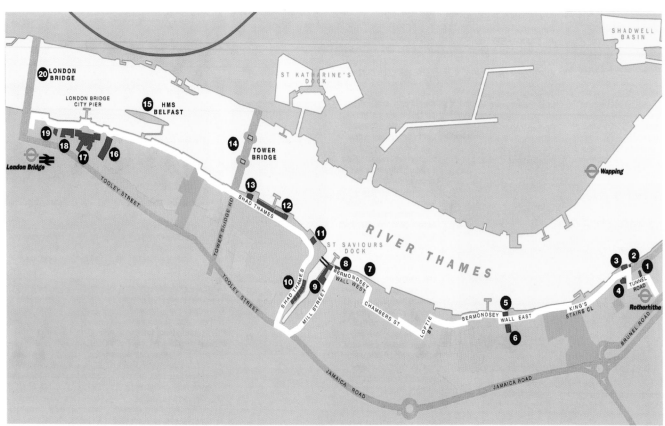

St Mary's Church (4) and
The Mayflower Pub (2).

The outstanding New Concordia Wharf apartments (9)
and new footbridge across St Saviour's Dock.

Restored schooners
at Bankside

An aerial view of London Docklands stretching from
Tower Bridge to Canary Wharf.

St James Church, Bermondsey.

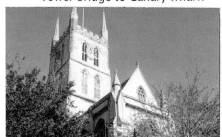

Southwark Cathedral dating
to the 12th century.

The historic Anchor Inn at Bankside.

Shakespeare's New Globe
Theatre at Bankside.

A replica of the Golden Hind
visiting London.

The Globe Theatre, New Tate Gallery, and the Millennium
Footbridge at Bankside.

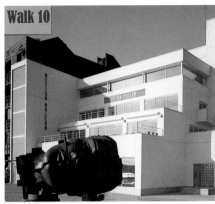

Design Museum (11) opened in 1989 at Butlers Wharf (12).

The Grade 2 listed Victorian warehouses in Butlers Wharf and the Anchor Brewhouse (13).

Shad Thames and Canyon Bridges at Butlers Wharf.

Mayor of London's new headquarters over-looking the Thames and Tower Bridge (14).

The view from Butlers Wharf riverside walkway showing the City, Tower Bridge and the Tower Hotel, on the north bank.

Top: Hayes Dock and wharf circa 1850s.
Left: Hayes Galleria (16) and The Horniman pub today.

The new Millennium Footbridge to St. Pauls.

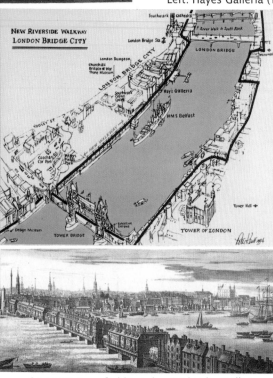

An engraving of old London Bridge by Hollar, with houses, shops and a chapel built on it.

The New Shakespeare Theatre at Bankside with 17th century London.

The Royal Docks Walk

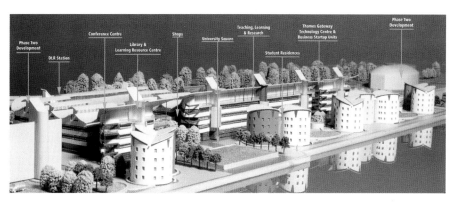

The Royal Docks

A few kilometres from the City lie the Royal Docks consisting of the Royal Victoria, Royal Albert and King George V Docks. They cover a huge area - the equivalent of Central London from Hyde Park to Tower Bridge and from Euston to Waterloo. Their immense size and shape make the Royals the most important city redevelopment site in Europe. Currently, it is virtually featureless apart from the University of East London campus and the London City Airport at the Royal Albert Dock.

Royal Victoria Dock

The enormous Royal Victoria Dock was the first of the Royals to be built in 1850-55, dug out by shovel and wheelbarrow. Sheds and silos were re-constructed during the 1920s and 1930s and the western entrance re-modelled during the early 1960s, but shortly afterwards it closed. In its heyday during the 19th century this was the largest enclosed dock system in the world. It functions with up to date hydraulic equipment and was the home of many ships from all over the world. Import cargo, such as meat, tobacco and tea, were discharged by dockers from ships to brick built warehouses, packaged and checked by Customs Officers and then transferred to railway wagons or road transport for inland distribution. Hundreds of barges carried goods to the riverside wharves right into the heart of the City. Export cargoes were delivered by rail or road to be loaded by stevedores into outward bound ocean-going ships or coastal steamers.

For over a century the Royal Docks were at the centre of the British Empire. Ships would be lined more than three deep and the quaysides echoed to the sounds of dockers as they loaded and discharged cargoes from all corners of the globe. Snapshots of these memories can be seen on the next page.

A glance at the map below reveals the few places to see around DLR stations on the north side of the docks. Pick up the DLR at Westferry or Blackwall station. The trains are computer controlled and driverless - they stop automatically if there is an obstruction on the line. The excellent feature of the railway is that most of the journey is at a high level providing splendid views over the docks. South of Royal Victoria station you will observe the colourful pumping station and the water sports centre at the western end of the Victoria Dock. Further along at Custom House are three listed Victorian Warehouses.

UEL Campus

The pride of the Royal Albert Dock is the new University Campus. Opened in September 1999, the University of East London Docklands Campus is the first of its kind in London for more than fifty years. Phase 1 occupies about half the 10 hectare site and offers courses in design, fine art, electrical and manufacturing engineering, cultural, media, communication and innovation studies. It also houses the Thames Gateway Technology Centre.

The campus has a public right of way running through the main square and along the dockside by the new international rowing course. The waterside walkway gives excellent views of the docks and airport. The main entrance to the campus is on foot from Cyprus DLR station. Prospective students are welcome to visit the Campus.

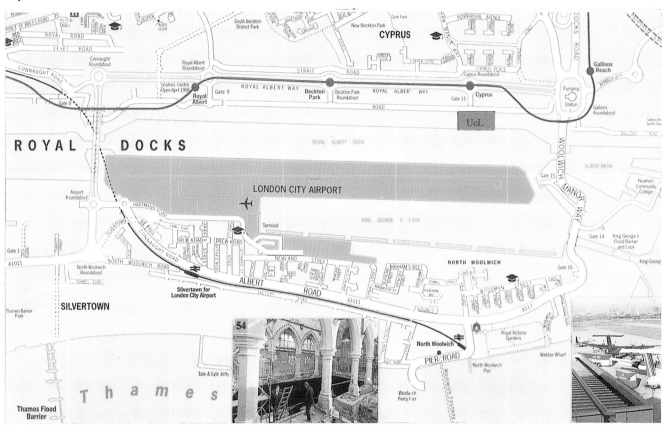

Police check point at the gate of
the Royal Albert Dock, c1960s.

Busy shipping scene at the Albert Dock, showing barrels
containing hide in brine imported from Australia, c1964.

Mechanical system for delivery of
bananas from ships to vans, c1960s.

This picture gives some idea of the huge goods
in the transit sheds of the Royal Docks, c1930s.

Great memories of the North Quay of the Albert Dock,
with stevedores discharging bags into a lighter, c1950s.

Tea bulking in a Port of London
Authority Warehouse, c1930.

New Zealand lamb being handled on the North
Quay of Albert Dock, c1960s.

Lamb carcasses being unloaded from the New Zealand
Ship Ranjitoto on North Quay of Albert Dock, c1996.

Top: Cars for Australian market standing on the quayside of the Victoria Dock during a strike
in 1965. Right: Aerial view of the Royal Docks, showing hardly a vacant berth, c1949.

Restored cranes on North Quay of Albert Dock, near the UEL Campus, provide a monument to Docklands history.

The new pride of the Royals is the University of East London Docklands Campus opened in September 1999, an aerial view looking north-east.

An aerial view showing the Victoria Dock in the foreground with a United States Line boat and the Albert Dock full of ships, c1960s.

The same quayside as above, with vessels being loaded for export using Stothart & Pitt cranes, c1966.

BT Earth Satellite station at North Woolwich.

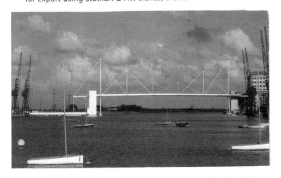

Spanning 130m across the Royal Victoria Dock, this footbridge provides a vital public access and an excellent infrastructure for the development of the area.

Top: The DLR Prince Regent Station opened 1994. Bottom: Britannia Village housing on the south side of Victoria Dock.

Modern pumping station resembling a ship, north of Victoria Dock.

The Manor Way level crossing of Beckton Railway, c1903, near the UEL Docklands Campus.

An aerial view of the Royal Docks looking west, showing London City Airport on the left and the site of the Docklands Campus near Gallions roundabout and drainage Pumping Station.

Royal Greenwich Walk

1. This walk starts at Island Gardens. Use the foot tunnel to cross under the river to Greenwich.

2. The Cutty Sark is a 19th century tea clipper which has been in the dry dock since 1954. You can wander on the upper and lower decks and there is an audio visual presentation of its history.

3. Gipsy Moth IV came to Greenwich in 1968 after being sailed single-handed around the world in 226 days by Sir Francis Chichester.

4. Former Royal Naval College is a fine and beautiful group of historical buildings started by Webb 1664 and developed by Wren 1692, Vanbrugh 1728 and the Chapel by Stuart 1789. It is the birth place of Henry VIII and his daughter Elizabeth I. See the magnificent painted Hall by Thornhall.

5. Further along the riverside is the Trafalgar Tavern, c1830s, a place where writers gathered including Charles Dickens who mentions the tavern in "Our Mutual Friend".

6. Proceed along Park Row to the Queen's House. Built by Inigo Jones this beautiful house was completed for the Queen of Denmark in 1619. The spectacular circular staircase resembles the one designed by Palladin in Venice.

7. The National Maritime Museum is one of the greatest museums in the world. It contains an extensive range of model ships, navigational instruments, naval weapons, uniforms and paintings.

8. St Alfage Church is a 17th century masterpiece by Hawksmoor and is dedicated to St Alfage. Following their raid to Canterbury in 1012, the Danes brought St Alfage to Greenwich and murdered him on the site of this church.

9. Greenwich market has a range of craft shops and is a place for browsing through books, jewellery and antiques during the weekends.

10. Return to Greenwich Park and walk uphill until you reach Flamstead House. This is the oldest part of the Royal Observatory and was the residence of the Astronomer Royal until 1948. The Octagon Room designed by Wren has been restored as it would have been in the 17th and 18th centuries with contemporary clocks and telescopes.

11. Old Royal Observatory is the home of Greenwich Mean Time where you can stand astride the Greenwich Meridian. The building was designed by Wren and built for King Charles II in 1658.

12. Blackheath is past Greenwich Park, where there are a number of restaurants, a golf club and a train station for your return to Central London.

The Great Hall in the Royal Naval College.

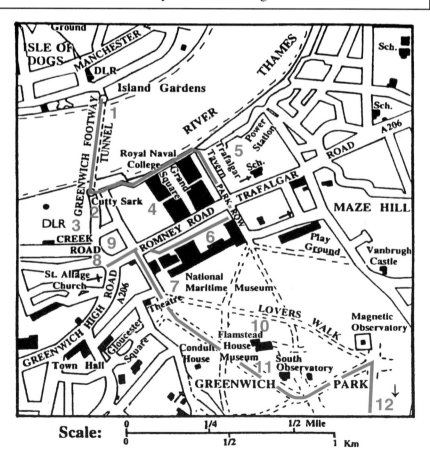

Scale:
0 — 1/4 — 1/2 Mile
0 — 1/2 — 1 Km

Bird's Eye view of Greenwich Pier, Cutty Sark, Royal Naval College, Queen's House, National Maritime Museum and Greenwich park.

Millennium Dome Walk | Walk 13 |

A zone by zone introduction to the Dome exhibitions and the Millennium Experience during year 2000. As well as the zones the visitor can enjoy the Millennium Show which runs up to six times a day, and takes place in the centre of the dome. Visitors arrive at North Greenwich Jubilee Line Station or by coach and the Dome is 1km in circumference.

Body

Measuring 64 metres from elbow to foot and 27 metres high, the giant abstract Body will amaze visitors. Combining two figures in a gentle reclining embrace, visitors will travel inside the Body and experience a multimedia show. They will then enter the Explore Area with its interactive exhibits on medical discoveries, lifestyle, health and beauty.

Sponsored by Boots with L'Oreal and Roche

Hayes Davidson

NMEC Anthony Pearson

Rest

Located on the inner ring of exhibition zones, Rest is located between the Our Town Story Theatre and Mind. With a bridge passing through the heart of its unique colourful structure, Rest will offer visitors a wonderfully contemplative environment in which to relax and reflect during their visit to the Dome.

Hayes Davidson

Faith

Six dramatic canopies stretch across a formation of 17m high arches. This beautiful structure will explore religious faith in the UK today, the Christian history and nature of our society and the varied multi-faith landscape of Britain.

Funded by charitable trusts.

Hayes Davidson

Self Portrait

A picture of the UK as it enters the next millennium, Self Portrait is a stunning 14m high circular structure. The revolving façade of the zone will feature the 'Andscape', a sequence of images nominated by the public, while the interior will house attractions by artist David Mach with his huge National Portrait collage and cartoonist Gerald Scarfe with his larger-than-life sculptures.

Sponsored by Marks & Spencer

Hayes Davidson

Home Planet

Visitors will be taken on a fantastic outer-space voyage departing, travelling and arriving at the most incredible planet in the universe - Earth. This journey takes place inside the shimmering blue attraction that will sit in the shadow of a giant globe floating high above visitors.

Sponsored by BAA and BA.

Shared Ground

The world's largest recycled cardboard structure, Shared Ground has captured the imagination of tens of thousands of British schoolchildren who have sent in the cardboard for the beautiful spiral shaped building. Celebrating the importance of community, the zone will take visitors on a journey contrasting the comfort of their own personal space with that of the shared ground of urban environments.

Sponsored by Camelot

Mind

With its continuously folding surfaces and 32m high central screen, the unique and bold architecture of Mind will amaze visitors. Featuring a series of exhibits - including new sculptures, optical illusions and breathtaking technology - the zone will combine Art and Science in its exploration of the Mind.

Sponsored by British Aerospace and GEC

Hayes Davidson

Journey

Journey is an architecturally dramatic zone with its series of angled fins that reach up to 25 metres in height. By entering at ground level visitors will ascend through the structure and explore the past, present and future of travel. Interactive displays and a virtual reality trip will feature in the zone.

Sponsored by Ford.

Money

With its glowing dramatic architecture, Money will entertain visitors and explain to them how money makes the world go round. Visitors will be able to play at being tycoons, react to the news in an interactive game and see how electronic cash is changing the way we spend and save.

Sponsored by City of London

Hayes Davidson

Work and Learning

With its huge 11m high rotating tryptych boards, Work and Learning will be the first zone that faces visitors as they enter the Dome. Learning - located on its upper floor - will take visitors on a journey from the school corridor of the past via an inspiring interactive film into the Learning Orchard of the Future.

Sponsored by Manpower and Tesco

NMEC/F15

Play

Located next to Body, Play will inevitably be one of the strongest attractions for the Dome's younger visitors. Brand new interactive games will be premiered inside the zone enabling visitors, whatever their age, the chance to participate and have fun.

NMEC Anthony Pearson

NMEC Sham

Living Island

Living Island will take visitors into a seaside environment complete with its own beach, promenade and games arcade. Entering the zone via a sewage pipe in the bottom of a recycled cliff, visitors will be able to explore the issues that affect our environment and discover through a variety of games just what a difference individual action can make.

Virtual Presence

32

North Bank Trail

Before the advent of the motor car and television, public houses were the centre of entertainment of the populace, especially in the area of the docks and along the Thames. They were places where the local residents went to spend some time to forget the back-breaking toil they performed in the docks. You can start this walk north of the Thames at Wapping tube station. The trail is clearly sign-posted all the way.

1   The first pub on the trail is the "Town of Ramsgate" which was probably serving some sort of ale during the Wars of the Roses c1440. A lot of water has flowed in the river since then. It is said the notorious Judge Jeffreys was caught here when he tried to escape to France from the wrath of the locals who had seen their friends strung up on the gallows behind the pub on sentence by the judge.

2   A short distance eastward and you find the "Captain Kidd" pub, so called because of the events which occurred nearby in 1701, when the famous pirate William Kidd was hung in Wapping then covered in tar and gibbeted in chains at Tilbury, as a warning to other would-be pirates.

3   In Wapping Wall by Shadwell Basin is probably the most famous pub the "Prospect of Whitby" with a beer garden overlooking the Thames. This 16th century pub boasts Pepys, Judge Jeffrey and the painter, Turner, amongst former regulars.

4   The "Barleymow" in Narrow Street, was originally a Dockmaster's house and stands at the entrance to Limehouse Basin.

5   Further along, among the 18th century sea captains' houses, is the "Grapes". Famous for its "Dickens" connection it has an old river balcony and a fish restaurant served from the nearby Billingsgate Fish Market.

6   A few doors away is "Booty"; this popular bar offers home cooked food all day until 9.30pm.

7   The "Henry Addington" at Canary Wharf, named after the Prime Minister who opened the West India Docks in 1802, is one of the new pubs. Located at the corner of the American Express building it has an American style bar.

8   The "Cat and Canary" is on the north side of the Tower and looks over the old West India Import Dock towards the magnificent converted Sugar Warehouses on the North Quay.

9   Facing the tall Cascade building is the "City Pride" pub. It has a large beer garden and is popular with office workers.

10 The "Waterfront" at South Quay Plaza overlooks the dock and has fine views of Canary Wharf. There is a high quality restaurant upstairs.

11 The "Gun" in Coldharbour on the east side of the Isle of Dogs was a handy meeting place for Lord Nelson with Lady Hamilton. It was also a resting place for lightermen waiting to dock their barges in the "West". They could take a leisurely pint on the veranda on the riverfront and keep their eye on their craft while they waited for the next lock-in. A long-gone coffee shop nearby served liver sandwiches during war rationing until the proprietor was summoned for selling horse-meat! During year 2000 there is a superb view of the Millennium Dome from this pub.

On the south side of the river walkers are familiar with the "Angel" (12) and Mayflower (13) pubs which are covered in the Docklands walks. The "Mayflower" in Rotherhithe is the place where the Pilgrim Fathers moored up their ship before setting sail for America in 1620.

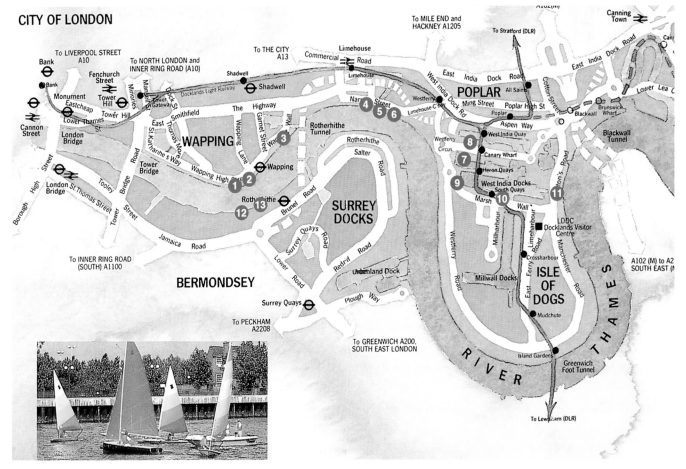

Isle of Dogs Historic Walk

This heritage trail is a journey in history of what you would have seen on the Isle of Dogs in the early 1980s before the regeneration. The trail started at Charlie Brown Pub (now demolished) at the junction of Westferry Road with East India Dock Road.

1 **Former Police Cottages** - Enter Garford Street where three cottages were built in 1819 by the West India Dock Company to house dock constables or police.

2 **Salvation Army Building** -This was first a mission to Scandinavian seamen until it was given to the Salvation Army in 1930.

3 **Dockmaster's House** - c1807, this was first used as an excise office, then became the Jamaica Tavern, reverted to a dock manager's office and is now a restaurant.

4 **Gate 1 and Piers** - The West India Import Dock was formerly surrounded by a ditch and railing c1803, the gate piers of which have survived.

5 **Ledger Building** - This was a general office until the closure of the docks.

6 **Warehouses 1 & 2** - As part of a group of nine which were ready to open with the dock in 1802. The interior was timber-framed but cast-iron columns were inserted in 1814.

7 **Round House** - Originally there were two buildings, one on either side of a gate out of the dock. One was used as a magazine for gun powder and the other as an overnight lock-up for thieves.

8 **Cannon Workshops** The central block, originally built around three sides of an open courtyard, was a cooperage with the other block built on the outside as a quadrangle for use as stores and workshops.

9 **West India Import & Export Docks** The Import Dock opened in 1802, the Export in 1806. The names of the two docks literally described their roles. There was room for 300, three-masted 300 ton vessels.

10 **South Dock & City Canal** - Built in 1805 the canal was designed as a short-cut on the long tidal haul around the southern end of the Isle of Dogs. In 1870 it was widened.

11 **Millwall Docks** - The Millwall Docks started off as a means of providing direct quay space for manufacturing including flour and timber mills.

12 **Pierhead Cottages** Built c1860 this group of buildings housed the dockmasters of the Millwall Dock Company (all demolished).

13 **Chapel, Westferry Road** - Built in 1856, the foundation stone was laid by John Scott Russell, builder of the Great Eastern. Formerly St Paul's Church it is now the Space Art Centre.

14 **Harbinger Primary School** - Built in 1904 and still in use this building is typical of its era. The original name, British Street Millwall School, is set in attractive tiles on the side facing Marsh Street.

15 **Burrell's Wharf** - The first site in the country laid out for large scale iron shipbuilding. The Great Eastern, built between 1853 and 1858, was one of the engineering wonders of the world.

16 **Ship Slipway** - the remains of one of the two 120ft long slipways was found in 1984.

17 **Building Plaque** - C J Mare and Company 1860 - marking Mare Millwall Ironwork.

18 **Cottages, Harbinger Road** Two terraces of cottages, some of the last surviving dockers' accommodation.

19 **Chapel House Estate** - George Lansbury cut the first turf for these post first world war "homes for heroes" in 1919. Named after the local medieval shrine, which was located on the site of the nearby graving dock, until it fell into ruins after the dissolution of the monasteries.

20 **Docklands Settlement** - As "The Welcome" this building opened in 1905 as a club and dining room for local factory girls.

21 **Railway Viaduct Millwall Park** - built in 1872 when the railway was extended south from Millwall Dock. The railway closed in 1926 but re-opened in 1987 as part of the new docklands light railway.

22 **Fire Station** - Another "Queen Anne" style building dating from 1904 and designed by the London County Council.

23 **The Lord Nelson** - Built c1859 the public house had a stabling block of 14 stalls. In 1899 the island boasted 40 "houses for sale of intoxicating drinks." In 1980 there were far less.

24 **Ferry House** - At one time this was the only building on the southern end of the Isle of Dogs apart from the Chapel House. It linked with the ferry and passengers from south of the river.

25 **Foot Tunnel** - Opened in 1902 the tunnel replaced the ferry and catered mainly for people working in the docks who lived in the Greenwich area.

26 **Island Gardens** - Viewed from Greenwich, the gardens were laid out by Poplar Borough Council.

27 **Newcastle draw dock** - Draw docks were used by small coasters and barges which would pull in at high tide for unloading into carts on the beach when it ebbed. This one was built c1850.

28 **Waterman's Arms** - An attractive building with wrought iron balconies, formerly known as the Newcastle Arms. The idea of enterprise zones was launched here at a dinner by the Rt.Hon Sir Geoffrey Howe MP.

29 **Christchurch** - Built in the 1850s, this church cost William Cubitt, the donor, some £7,000.

30 **Mudchute** - The silted mud from the Millwall Dock was mixed with water and forced by compressed air into settling beds. Now the mud has solidified and grass has grown. Cows and sheep graze and children enjoy one of London's popular urban farms.

31 **Site of rope walk** - Formerly the Globe Rope Works, this site includes the rail tracks used by rope-laying machines.

32 **Carnegie Public Library** - An Edwardian stone building, c1904, with timber cupola.

33 **Fred Olsen Building** - The staff amenity and operational control building, opened in 1970.

34 **Blue Bridge** - Large modern Dutch-style draw bridge built by the Port of London Authority in 1969

35 **The Gun** - One of the oldest pubs on the river but altered in the 19th century. It provides sweeping views of the Blackwall Reach.

36 **Isle House & Nelson House** - Nelson House and the two northern-most houses in Coldharbour date from the early 19th century.

37 **Bridge House** - This fine house was built in 1819 for the superintendent of the West India Dock Company.

38 **Poplar Railway Dock** - Built in 1830, it was leased in 1850 to the North London Railway Company and enlarged to form a dock for the coal trade. The two towers housed hydraulic accumulators.

39 **Hydraulic Pumping Station** - Built in the late 19th century, this station provided hydraulic power to operate cranes and lock gates in the nearby Midland Railway Dock at Polar Dock.

Pictures of past and present Isle of Dogs are given on pages 36 and 37.

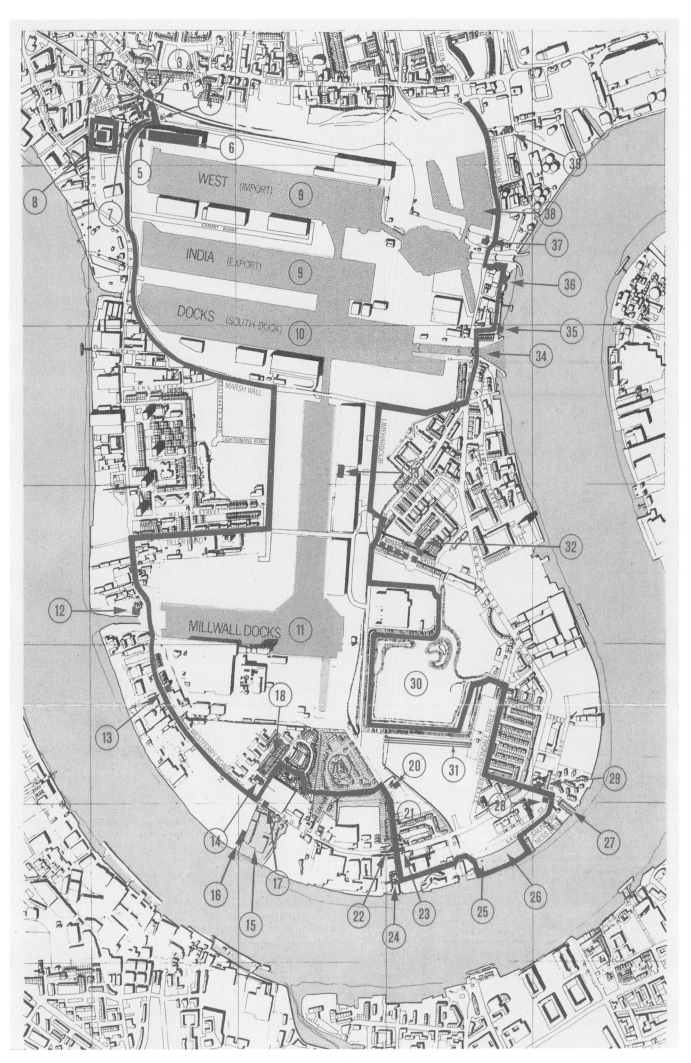

The magnificent warehouses on the North Quay of the Import Dock circa1802

Left: Maps of Isle of Dogs circa 1755 and 1929.

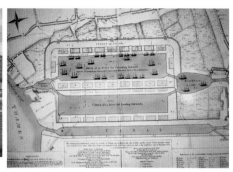

Plan of the West India Import and Export Docks circa 1802 showing the nine warehouses.

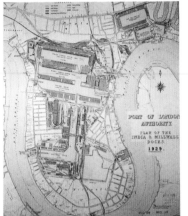

Aerial view of the derelict Isle of Dogs circa 1983 with the old Canary Wharf at the centre.

The old M Shed completed in 1966 with a ramp for lorries on the South Quay, circa 1985.

Aerial view of Canary Wharf looking west circa 1980s.

Views of the old derelict North Quay Warehouses 1 and 2 circa early 1980s. These have now been renovated and converted into apartments and accommodation for housing the Museum of Docklands.

McDougalls silos and Timber Wharves on south side of Millwall Outer Dock (demolished).

The old sheds on the North Quay of the Import Dock circa mid 1980s (demolished).

A view of the old Heron Quay and Canary Wharf sheds from the South Quay, circa 1980s.

The old Canary Wharf sheds overlooking the Export Dock circa mid 1980s (demolished).

The historic Cannon Workshops circa 1824, now converted into commercial units.

Isle of Dogs past

A view of old Canary Wharf showing the derelict Shed No. 10 left and others circa mid 1980s.

Cabot Square at Canary Wharf.

South Quay Development, c1994.

New pontoon footbridge connecting Canary Wharf to North Quay and Docklands Museum.

View from Island Gardens of Trafalgar Tavern and the Royal Naval College.

Pier Lock development and Blue Bridge, c2000.

The new hotel on South Quay.

Aerial view of Cannon Workshop at the West India Dock conservation area.

A view of the Millennium Dome and Canary Wharf looking west toward the City.

Limehouse Link tunnel.

The DLR extended to Lewisham, c2000.

A view of Millwall Dock developments showing Docklands Light Railway (DLR).

Glengall Bridge development and crossing.

Cabot Square fountain.

Tower from West India Avenue.

Spectacular Christmas lights c1995.

Night view of Lower Lea River crossing.

Isle of Dogs present

The Cascade apartments, west side of the Isle of Dogs, c1998.

Royal Westminster Walk

1. Start your walk at Trafalgar Square where you see Lord Nelson's statue c1840, the National Gallery and the Church of St Martin-in-the-Fields, c1721.
2. The Admiralty Arch was erected as a memorial to Queen Victoria.
3. Old Scotland Yard.
4. Proceed along Whitehall and the Admiralty Building, c1726, is on your right.
5. Ministry of Agriculture.
6. A boat converted into a restaurant.
7. A green resting place overlooking the Embankment and River Thames.
8. Banqueting House, a palace of 1622 with magnificent ceiling paintings by Rubens. From here Charles I was taken to execution.
9. Horse Guards, the sentries of the Royal Household Cavalry.
10. The Prime Minister's residence at No 10 Downing Street, since 1732.
11. The British Empire's war memorial - Cenotaph, c1920.
12. The Foreign Office building.
13. The Treasury building.
14. Big Ben, the Clock Tower, is lit when Parliament is in session.
15. The magnificent Victorian Gothic style Houses of Parliament, c1858, Westminster Hall and House of Lords.
16. Victoria Tower and Gardens overlooking the Thames.
17. The Jewel Tower, Edward III's treasure house.
18. Westminster Abbey nearly 1000 years old and the place of coronation of English kings. Make a brass rubbing as a souvenir.
19. St Margaret's Church of 12th century origin.
20. Go around Parliament Square into Great George Street and you can visit Churchill's War Room Museum - underground.
21. Birdcage Walk where a royal aviary was created by King James I.
22. Enter St James's Park which dates back to the 16th century and has a large bird population around the lake.
23. Queen Victoria's Memorial, c1911, stands outside Buckingham Palace, where the Queen's Gallery exhibits treasures from the Royal collection.
24. Changing the Guard takes place daily about 11.00 am. Adjoining is the Royal Mews for the Royal coaches and horses.
25. Proceed to The Mall and Lancaster House, c1827, was built for the Duke of York.
26. Clarence House is the residence of the Queen Mother. Turn left through Stable Yard into Pall Mall.
27. Turn right into Pall Mall. St James's Palace, built by Henry VIII as the Official Court of the Sovereign.
28. York House is the formal residence of the Duke and Duchess of York.
29. Gainsborough's house at No 80 Pall Mall.
30. Marlborough House built by Wren for the Duke of Marlborough, the ancestor of Winston Churchill.
31. Pall Mall's stately clubs are situated here, including the Athenaeum (1823), Travellers Club, Reform Club, and United Service (1815).
32. Turn right into Waterloo Place. Carlton House Terrace is one of the most aristocratic residences in London. Napoleon III lived at No 1, now the residence of the Foreign Secretary. Lord Kitchener's house was No 2. Lord Palmerston was at No 4. The world famous Royal Society is centred at No. 6. No 11 was Lord Gladstone's residence in 1857.
33. Statue of Duke of York.

LONDON WALKS
Start from this page

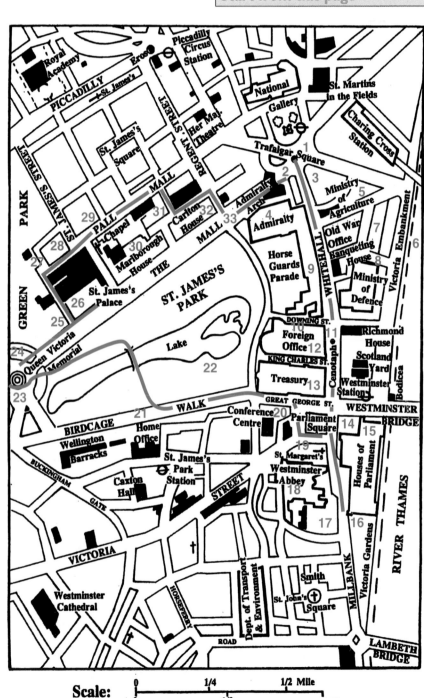

Scale: 0 — 1/4 — 1/2 Mile
0 — 1/2 — 1 Km

Whitehall in Westminster, the seat of the British Government, stretches from Trafalgar Square to Parliament Square.

London West End Walk

1. Start from Trafalgar Square walking east along the Strand. Charing Cross Station is a major terminal for London commuters.

2. Gordon's Wine Bar at No 47 Villiers Street, has a trade charter issued in 1364.

3. Pepys lived at No 12 Buckingham Street. At the end of the street is Watergate, which was the riverbank before the development of the Victoria Embankment in the 1860s.

4. In Adelphi Terrace lived Dickens, Garrick and George Bernard Shaw.

5. Chapel of the Savoy, c1505, was built on the site of a 13th century palace.

6. London Transport Museum has exciting exhibitions on the history and development of transport. There is also a well-stocked book shop.

7. Covent Garden is a fashionable area of Central London with shops and cafés to provide a pleasurable place for Londoners and visitors.

8. The Church of St Paul's, c1638, on the north side of the square has associations with artists and actors.

9. The Royal Opera House was commissioned by Charles II in 1660 and has recently been rebuilt.

10. St Mary-le-Strand church, c1714, where Thomas Becket was lay rector.

11. India House and Australia House at Aldwych, which is Danish in origin, probably due to a settlement there. The area has a number of well-known theatres.

    Just north of Aldwych in Portsmouth Street is the Old Curiosity Shop built in 1567 and made famous by Charles Dickens in his book bearing the same name. It is currently used as an antique and art shop.

12. St Clement Danes Church, built by Wren in 1680.

13. Royal Courts of Justice (The Law Courts) was built in 1882 with public galleries. The Central Hall has a fine mosaic floor. Guided tours can be arranged.

14. Temple Bar in Fleet Street marks the western boundary of the City of London.

15. Public Record Office in Chancery Lane with documents dating to the Domesday Book of 1086.

16. St Dunstan in the West, c1671, with a clock and statue of King Lund.

17. Childs Bank was established in 1671.

18. Prince Henry's Room is in a timber-framed building, 17 Fleet Street, dating back to 1611 which was used as a tavern.

19. Inns of Court of 13th century origin is the prestigious centre for the legal profession.

20. Temple Church has its origin with the Crusaders, Knight Templers of 1165. Chapel added 1240.

21. Ye Olde Cock Tavern.

22. Hoare's Bank at No 37 Fleet Street privately owned Bank since 1672

23. Dr Johnson's residence during 1749-1758, entrance from 147 Fleet Street.

24. The Cheshire Cheese Pub rebuilt 1667 where Dr Johnson, Boswell and Oliver Goldsmith drank.

25. St Bride Church built by Wren in 1671 on the site of a Norman church.

26. Old Bailey, the main criminal court in Britain, the site dating to 1539 but rebuilt in 1907.

27. St Paul's Cathedral was completed in 1710 by Wren after the Great Fire of 1666. Its design resembles St Peters in Rome but on a significantly smaller scale.

28. Tourists Information Centre. To the north of the Cathedral is St Paul's tube station for return to your destination.

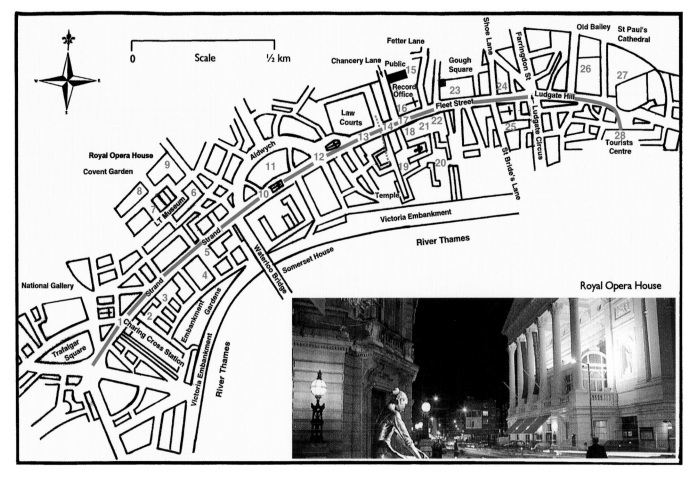

Royal Opera House

Aerial view of Trafalgar Square looking north showing the National Gallery, Church of St Martins-in-the-Field, Nelson's Column and Admiralty Arch. The Strand is shown top right.

A view of the City skyline and St Paul's Cathedral across the Thames with Blackfriars Bridge in the foreground.

The Plaza at Covent Garden, a shopping precinct for fashion and crafts, with restaurants and cafés.

A view of Charing Cross Pier and railway station along the Victoria Embankment with Whitehall to the left.

The Royal Courts of Justice, Law Courts, in the Strand, with galleries for the public to view the proceedings.

Leicester Square & Soho Walk

1. Start at Trafalgar Square the home of the National Gallery housing one of the greatest art collections in the world.

2. Enter St Martin's Place where on the corner is St Martin-in-the-Fields church, c1721.

3. National Portrait Gallery has thousands of portraits, paintings, sculptures and fine drawings.

4. London Coliseum Theatre is the home of the English National Opera.

5. The Salisbury Pub frequented by theatrical people.

6. The Hippodrome for disco and music.

7. Leicester Square with its famous Odeon Cinema, the Empire, the Swiss Centre and many more attractions and bars.

8. The Trocadero, a centre for exhibitions, restaurants and music shops. Turn right into Windmill Street and right again into Shaftesbury Avenue.

9. Pass the Globe Theatre and turn left into Greek Street reaching Soho Square, one of the most elegant places in London. The surrounding Georgian mansions are occupied by high society including Dukes and Ambassadors. There are Chinese and continental restaurants in the area.

10. North-east of Soho Square is Tottenham Court Road with its high rise Centre Point office block.

11. Mozart lived at No 20 Frith Street and taught at No 22.

12. Karl Marx lived at No 26 Dean Street.

13. Blue Posts Pub is in Rupert Street. Turn right and walk along Brewer Street and right again into James Street.

14. Golden Square, a green resting area with benches.

15. Carnaby Street, one of the most fashionable areas for clothes in the world. At the top of Carnaby Street turn left and left again into Regent Street.

16. London Diamond Centre and Exhibition is at No 10 Hanover Street.

17. At the corner of Regent Street is Liberty, famous for clothes, fabrics etc. Other shops include Jaeger at No 204 for tweeds, woollens, etc. Scotch House at No 191 for Shetlands etc. Gerrard at No 112 are the Crown Jewellers.

18. Café Royal is an upperclass place for more than a hundred years with function rooms for weddings etc.

19. Piccadilly Circus is the West End top tourist centre, surrounded by many famous London theatres.

20. Burberry's coats and woollens in Haymarket.

21. American Express main office in London. At the end of Haymarket turn left into Pall Mall and return to Trafalgar Square.

Carnaby Street in Soho, one of the most fashionable areas for clothes in the world since 1957.

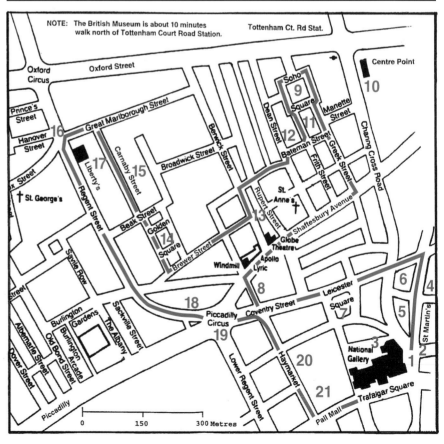

An elevated view of Piccadilly Circus in the heart of London's West End, with the statue of Eros in the centre.

An aerial view of Soho Square (top left) and Tottenham Court Road area with the spectacular 35-storey office block Centre Point, built in 1966.

St James's & Mayfair Walk

1 From Piccadilly Circus enter Regent Street, turn right into Pall Mall then right into St James's Square. No 31 was owned by the Dukes of Norfolk and was the birthplace of George III.

2 No 32 was the former residence of the Bishops of London.

3 Statue of William III, c1808.

4 No. 10 was the former home of three Prime Ministers - Chatham, Gladstone and Lord Derby.

5 No 14 Carlisle's Private Library c1841, used by writers Dickens, George Elliot and Thackeray.

6 No 8 King Street is Christie's, the world renowned auctioneers since 1766.

7 Sir Thomas More and Hayden lived at No 1 Bury Street.

8 At No 3 are the wine sellers, Berry Bros and Rudd since 1699.

9 Pickering Place was the Quarters of the Republic of Texas involved in legation during 1842-45.

10 James Lock & Co, master hat makers since 1759 with a showroom for period items.

11 Edward Gibbon lived at No 2 in 1766.

12 Byron, the poet, lived at No 8 St James's Street

13 Exclusive clubs based at St James's Street include the Carlton (No 69).

14 A short detour to St James's Park is delightful with magnificent views of Buckingham Palace and Whitehall from the bridge across the lake.

15 Return to the end of St James's Street. You can either turn right into Piccadilly and along on your left are the Arcade Shopping Precinct, the Royal Academy of Arts and the Museum of Mankind. Old Bond Street leads to New Bond Street where you will find a great variety of shops for fashionable clothes, leather, china, etc. Sothebys, the well-known auctioneers are at No 35, Lord Nelson lived at No 147 and Lady Hamilton at No 150. In Brook Street Handel lived at No 25. At the top of the road is Oxford Street.

16 Alternatively, turn left into Piccadilly and enter White Horse Street. Shepherd Market is a colourful part of Mayfair with pubs and restaurants.

17 General Burgoyne lived at No 10 till 1792 and Sheridan 1795 to 1802.

18 Disraeli died at No 19 Curzon Street.

19 Red Lion Pub, a quiet place dating back to Victorian times.

20 Berkeley Square is a beautiful green place with plane trees planted in 1789. Sir Winston Churchill lived at No 48 during his childhood. William Pitt, another Prime Minister, lived at No 47 and Lord Clive of India committed suicide at No 45.

Selfridge's, the impressive department store in Oxford Street, has everything for the ladies and their family needs.

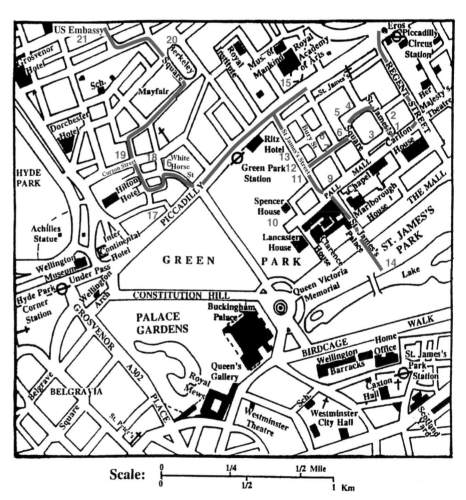

Scale: 0 — 1/4 — 1/2 Mile / 0 — 1/2 — 1 Km

21 Grosvenor Square is the home of the American Embassy built in 1958. John Adams, past US President, lived at No.9 when he was Ambassador. Roosevelt Memorial is in the square

Walk a short distance along North Audley Street and you reach Oxford Street, famous for its fashion shops etc. Directly facing you is Selfridges, an impressive department store opened by an American millionaire, Gordon Selfridge, in 1909.

Aerial view looking north of St James's Square, The Mall, St James's Park, Admiralty Arch and Trafalgar Square.

View of St James's Square and the Duke of York statue, looking south toward the park and the Houses of Parliament. This square and the surrounding areas show affluence of 18th and 19th century London.
Insets: Houses of Parliament and Trafalgar Square.

Buckingham Palace, the Queen's London home, as viewed from the bridge in St James's Park.

Bird's eye view of the American Embassy in Grosvenor Square, where there is a memorial to President Roosevelt.

View of Whitehall and the lake as viewed from the bridge in St James's Park.

Marylebone & London Zoo

1. Start your walk at Marble Arch station. Designed by John Nash c1828, the Arch was originally the gateway to Buckingham Palace and was moved to its present position. It is the site of the old Tyburn Gallows. On the other side of the green is Speakers Corner where the general public profess their views on Sundays without hindrance

2. Proceed eastward along Oxford Street until you reach the Edwardian building of superstore Selfridge's. It has numerous departments especially for ladies. Further along Oxford Street there are other superstores.

3. Baker Street is associated with the fictitious detective, Sherlock Holmes, and his assistant Dr Watson,who were supposed to have lodged at No 221B, now owned by the Halifax Building Society. Running parallel is Harley Street with private medical consulting rooms.

4. The Wallace Collection in Manchester Square, off Baker Street, has a permanent exhibition of paintings, French furniture and armour.

5. At the top of Baker Street, turn right into Marylebone Road and the Planetarium dome will be facing you. The Zeiss Star Projector takes you through time and space in daily shows. In the evening laser light concerts are held.

6. Madame Tussauds Waxworks museum opened in London c1835. The exhibitions show past and present world personalities, including the royalty, statesmen, politicians, sport and entertainment stars.

7. The Royal Regent Park is one of the finest in Central London and contains the London Zoo. Designed by John Nash during 1812-26. During the 16th century, it was part of Henry VIII's hunting forests. The Queen Mary's Rose Garden proves a perfect place to relax and there is an open-air theatre.

8. London Zoo, laid out in 1827, is one of the largest and most famous zoos in the world containing a huge collection of animals including the giant panda. Feeding time for the lions and tigers is an exciting spectacle. The Aquarium and the Apes and Monkeys Pavilions display animals from many continents.

9. London Central Mosque, situated on the edge of the Park, has the largest golden dome in the UK.

10. Take either a relaxing Regent Canal boat trip in the park or return to Marylebone Road and walk eastwards to Cleveland Street. The British Telecom Tower, 177m high, gives excellent views over London.

The Wallace Collection in Manchester Square is a permanent exhibition of paintings, French furniture and armour.

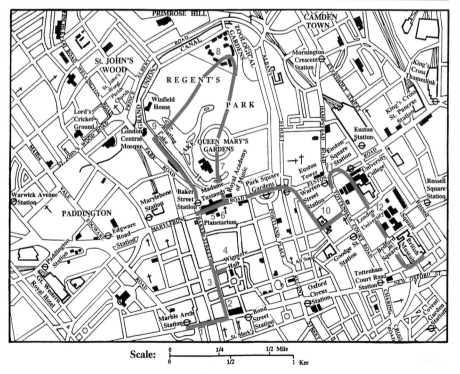

Scale:

11. Walking towards Euston and Kings Cross Stations, you reach the great New British Library at 96 Euston Road, NW1, housing over 12 million books.

12. Nearby in Gower Street is University College and London University in Russell Square. The superb British Museum is in Russell Street.

The Planetarium and Madame Tussauds Waxworks Museum in Marylebone Road, near Baker Street tube station.

The beautiful Rose Garden near the York Gate of Regents Park.

Marble Arch and Hyde Park Speakers Corner at the top of Oxford Street. The Odeon Cinema (black) is above the tube station.

The bridge and island by the east side of Queen Mary's Gardens at Regents Park.

Top: John Lewis super store in Oxford Street, has a wide range of goods for the family and household. The partnership started in 1864 with one shop specialising in textiles which is still the most important part of their retail business Left: The tall British Telecom Tower houses telecommunication equipment with a revolving top and a sight-seeing gallery giving spectacular panoramic views of London since the early 1960s.

1. This walk starts at Hyde Park Corner. The statue of the Duke of Wellington was erected in 1888. The Duke rides his favourite horse 'Copenhagen'.
2. Apsley House is where the Duke of Wellington lived and is now a museum containing paintings, silverware and military relics
3. High-rise Hilton Hotel overlooking Hyde Park.
4. Royal Artillery Memorial erected in 1925 to those who lost their lives during World War I.
5. Harvey Nichols is a super store of ladieswear, cosmetics, menswear etc.
6. Harrods is the world-renowned store and centre of excellent fashion and selection of high quality goods.
7. Roman Catholic Church in Italian style with notable interior carvings and mosaic.
8. Victoria and Albert Museum opened by Edward VII in 1909 as a national museum of applied arts including superb paintings, sculpture, costumes, fabrics, jewellery, tapestry and woodwork.
9. Islamic Cultural Centre for Ismaili Muslim Community.
10. Natural History Museum, Gothic style c1881, houses both the national collection of botany & zoology and the largest geology collection of gems, precious stones and fossils in the world.
11. Science Museum in Exhibition Road is an outstanding museum which tells the story of science applied to industry, with models, steam engines, motor cars, space capsules and many aspects of engineering, physics and chemistry.
12. Imperial College of Science, Medicine and Technology, established in 1907 for advanced training and research.
13. Royal Albert Hall, opened in 1871 by Queen Victoria in memory of her husband, is the venue for pop and classical concerts, conferences and rallies. The Royal Geographic Society is nearby.
14. Cross Kensington Road to see the Albert Memorial in Hyde Park, erected in 1876 as a sculpture of metal, mosaic, gilt and enamel which has recently been renovated.
15. Serpentine Gallery provides a platform for young artists during the summer.
16. Peter Pan is a superb statue erected in 1912 for children.
17. Royal Kensington Palace was upgraded by Wren to a palace in 1689 for William III. It was the home of Diana, the Princess of Wales, until her tragic death in a car accident in Paris. The Court Dress Collection is open to the public as is Kensington Gardens.

Aerial view of the museums in South Kensington.

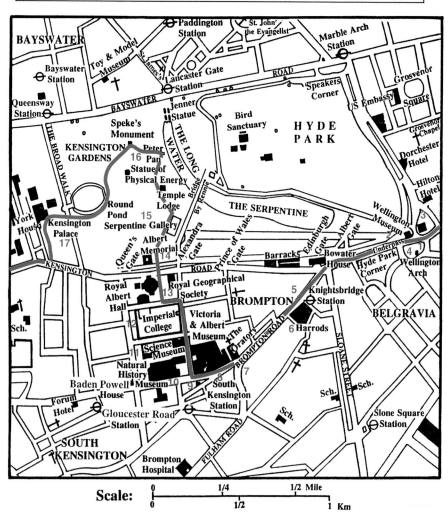

Scale:
0   1/4   1/2 Mile
0   1/2   1 Km

Re-join Kensington Road and walk west to High Street Kensington for restaurants, cafés, and fashionable shops including Barkers and a jewellery arcade.

From here you can walk along Church Street and get to Notting Hill Gate. A short walk westward leads to the Portobello Road Market world-famous for antiques.

The Albert Memorial in Hyde Park and the Royal Albert Hall were both erected in memory of Queen Victoria's husband.

Diana, the late Princess of Wales, lived in Kensington Palace.

Harrods of Knightsbridge the world-famous departmental store and centre of excellence for high quality goods.

Kensington Palace, was upgraded to a palace for William III in 1689. Queen Victoria was born here in 1819.

A short walk from Kensington High Street is the world-famous antique market in Portobello Road, with fruit and vegetable stalls, located in a narrow and crowded street off Westbourne Park.

South Bank Riverside Walk

Start the Thames Path walk along the South Embankment from Lambeth Bridge.

1   The medieval Lambeth Palace has been the London seat of the Archbishop of Canterbury since 1197. The Great Hall contains portraits from the 16th to 19th century.

2   The Museum of Garden History is housed in the church adjacent to Lambeth Palace. The churchyard has the grave of Captain Bligh of the Mutiny on the Bounty.

3   A short detour along Lambeth Road brings you to the Imperial War Museum which contains extensive exhibits of warfare.

4   St Thomas's Hospital and Medical School have modern buildings but the site dates back to 1106. There are beautiful views of the Houses of Parliament from the South Bank.

5   Former County Hall was the seat of the London County Council for over one hundred years and was sold after the demise of the Greater London Council in March 1986. It has been converted into a hotel and an aquarium.

6   The London Eye, or the Millennium Wheel, completed in January 2000, is the largest Ferris Wheel in the world. The ride takes about half an hour giving magnificent views over London, (p62).

7   This high-rise concrete building is the former Shell Centre and was completed in 1962.

8   South Bank Arts Complex includes the Festival Hall, the Queen Elizabeth Hall, the National Theatre and the Hayward Gallery, all originated in the Festival of Britain of 1951.

9   Royal Festival Hall opened in 1951, hosts a variety of concerts and plays.

10 Hayward Gallery provides a series of exhibition galleries and a sculpture hall.

11 Museum of the Moving Image, established in 1989, is the world's largest museum devoted to cinema and television.

12 Royal National Theatre is well-known for English plays including Macbeth by Shakespeare.

13 Further along the river are the impressive London Weekend Television building, the fine art deco OXO Tower, illuminated at night, and the Sea Container House with its gold leaf balls dominating the vista.

Bankside is the last destination on this walk where the New Tate Gallery and the New Shakespeare Globe Theatre have recently been completed. The delightful 17th century riverside Anchor Inn provides a perfect place for your journey's end.

The Festival Hall Pier at Waterloo Bridge for pleasure boat trips.

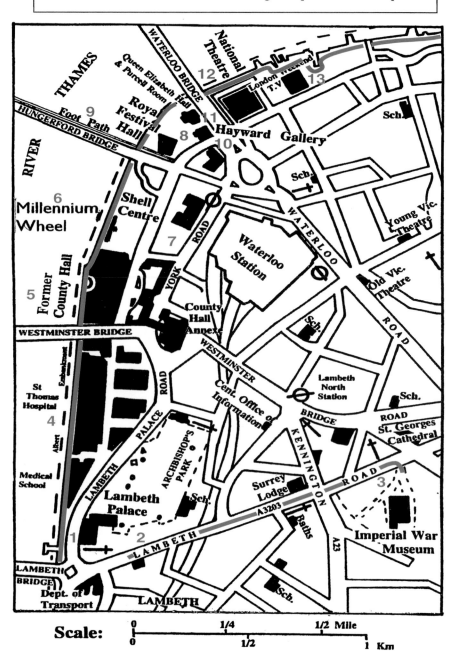

Scale:

| 0 | 1/4 | 1/2 Mile |
| 0 | 1/2 | 1 Km |

The former London County Hall, recently converted into a hotel and aquarium, still retains the original oak-panelled splendour of 1922.

An aerial view looking north, c1992, shows the north and south banks from Lambeth Bridge to Waterloo Bridge. Lambeth Palace and St Thomas's Hospital are seen bottom right of the picture.

City & Bank of England

The following walk starting from Bank Station takes about an hour and a half and covers two and a half kilometres.

1 **Bank of England & Museum** - Founded in 1694 to finance the war against Louis XIV of France, it has since become the bank of government and the nation. The present building, designed by Sir Herbert Baker, was completed in 1937. The adjacent museum tells the story of the bank.

2 **Royal Exchange** - Founded by Sir Thomas Gresham in 1566, the present building was designed by Sir William Tate in 1844. Used as an exchange for merchants for four centuries, it is now occupied by insurance organisations.

3 **Building 33-35 Cornhill** - Ornate classical building of Portland stone completed in 1857.

4 **Simpsons Tavern** - An old tavern located in an area of alleyways.

5 **Church of St Michael** - Built by Wren 1670-2, except for the tower.

6 **Church of St Peter** - By Wren 1677-81, the churchyard contains two London plane trees.

7 **Building 140-144 Leadenhall Street** - Designed by Lutyens, this Portland stone building dates to 1929.

8 **P & O, and Commercial Union** - The two modern buildings by Melvin Ward were built 1964-9.

9 **Church of St Helen** - This is the remains of a Benedictine nunnery.

10 **Church of St Andrew Undershaft** - The name comes from the shaft of the maypole. The tower and church were built during 15th and 16th centuries.

11 **Lloyd's Building** - The international and world-famous insurance market, the new building on the east side of Lime Street, was erected by Heysham 1950-57 and is connected by a bridge to the old headquarters by Sir Edwin Cooper 1925-28.

12 **Office Block 34-36 Lime Street** - The building by Sheppard and Robson was completed in 1974.

13 **Leadenhall Market** - The Victorian retail market by Sir Horace Jones 1881, has shops devoted to the food trade. Beneath the market archaeologists found the site of the Roman Basilica.

14 **Building 2-3 Philpot Lane** - In the Court at the rear of No.1 you find a much altered 18th century building.

15 **Building 4,7 and 18 Philpot Lane** - This is a late 17th century 4-storey building.

16 **Building 223-25 Eastcheap** - A mid 19th century corner building of polychrome brick.

17 **Building 33-35 Eastcheap** - a Gothic design built in 1877.

18 **Church of St Mary-at-the-Hill** Built by Wren 1670-76 to replace an older church first mentioned in 1177.

19 **One Tree Park** - The area is frequented by traders.

20 **The Monument** - Designed by Wren, and erected in 1671-77 to commemorate the Great Fire of 1666. The height of 61m is the distance westward from the baker's shop in Pudding Lane where the fire started.

21 **Church of St. Edmund the King** - built by Wren 1670-79.

22 **Building 60-62 Lombard Street** - Early 20th century construction.

23 **Church of St Mary Woolnoth** - Built by Hawksmoor 1716-27.

24 **Building 1 Cornhill** - Recent design building of Portland stone with rounded corner supporting a dome.

25 **Mansion House** - Official residence of the Lord Mayor of the City of London during his year of office.

Leadenhall Market.

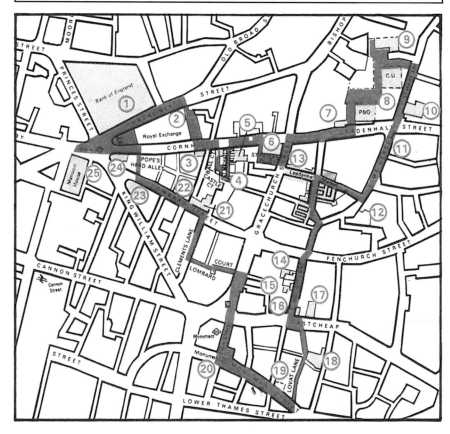

The Monument c1677, with excellent views of the City.

The interior of Mansion House, the official residence of the Lord Mayor of the City of London during his year of office.

St Pauls Cathedral from the river.

Left: The Victorian Leadenhall Market. Middle: The modern architecture of Lloyds of London, the international and world famous insurance market, building erected in 1987.
Right: The Bank of England, founded 1694, and museum which tells its history.
Below left and right: The ever changing scene of the Royal Exchange and Bank of England, shown as they are today and as they were at the end of 19th century.

City & St Paul's Cathedral

This walk around St Paul's is about 4km long and takes about 2 hours.

26 **St Paul's Cathedral -** the original Cathedral was founded in AD604 and rebuilt in stone by the Saxons.

27 **Chapter House -** Built by Wren 1712-14 and repaired after the war.

28 **Paternoster Precinct** - re-developed 1961-67 and 2000.

29 **Tower and remains of Christchurch -** On the site of the Chancel of the Franciscan (Greyfriars) Church.

30 **National Postal Museum -** Contains Phillips collection of 19th century British postal stamps from 1840.

31 **Statue of Rowland Hill** -Founder of penny post, by Onslow Ford 1881.

32 **Postman's Park -** Contains Minotaur sculpture by Michael Ayrton, and a memorial shelter.

33 **Church of St Botolph, Aldersgate -** Founded before 1291 and rebuilt 1791.

34 **Gateway Leading into Churchyard -** Has picturesque upper storeys.

35 **Church of St Bartholomew-the-Great** - In 1123 Rahere, a prebendary of St Paul's, founded St Bartholomew's .

36 **Drinking Fountain -** Bronze female figure by J B Philip dated1873.

37 **43-45 Cloth Fair -** Late 18th century houses and shop fronts.

38 **41-42 Cloth Fair -** Much restored late 17th century houses.

39 **Smithfield Market -** Designed by Sir Horace Jones c1868 and owned by the Corporation of London.

40 **Hand and Shears Public House -** Early 19th century corner building.

41 **Museum of London -** Designed by Powell and Moya 1974 houses the greatest collections on London.

42 **Barbican -** The centre for Arts and Conferences, the largest in Europe. *Barbican* means a projecting watch tower over the gate of a fortified town.

43 **Roman Wall -** Sections of the wall on the north side of London Wall.

44 **Church of St Giles Cripplegate -** It stands in the middle of the Barbican area and was restored after war damage.

45 **Upper level walkway -** A link to major centres in the City.

46 **Exhibition Hall -** An exhibition featuring aspects of City life.

47 **Sculpture -** Beyond Tomorrow by Karin Jonzen, 1972.

48 **Glass Fountain -** by Alan David.

49 **Stainless Steel Sculpture -** Ritual by Antanas Brazdys, 1969.

50 **Guildhall -** Centre of the City's government for more than 1,000 years.

51 **Church of St Lawrence Jewry** - 1671-87 by Wren. Following war damage the church was restored in 1954-57 by Cecil Brown.

52 **Irish Chamber -** Early 19th century corner building of yellow brick and stucco.

53 **42-44 Gresham Street -** Italianate corner building of Portland stone c1850.

54 **3 King Street -** Distinguished classical design by Thomas Hopper in 1836.

55 **Church of St Mary-le-Bow -** Another Wren church built 1670-83.

56 **6-8 Bow Lane -** Mid 19th century commercial building of polychrome brick.

57 **24-26 Watling Street -** Mid 19th century commercial building.

58 **19-21 Watling Street -** Mid 19th century building of yellow brick and stone.

59 **Festival Gardens -** Constructed at the time of the Festival of Britain in 1951.

60 **Tower of Church of St Augustine -** 1680-83 by Wren. The graceful spire has been reconstructed following war damage.

61 **St Paul's Cathedral Choir School -** Designed by Leo de Syllas of the Architect's Co-Partnership, 1962-7.

62 **St Paul's Cross -** Rebuilt 1910 to mark the site of a preaching cross.

63 **Church of St Mary Aldermary -** Wren rebuilt the church in 1682 after the Great Fire.

64 **Remains of the Temple of Mithras -** Foundations of temple to a Roman Sun God were discovered in 1954.

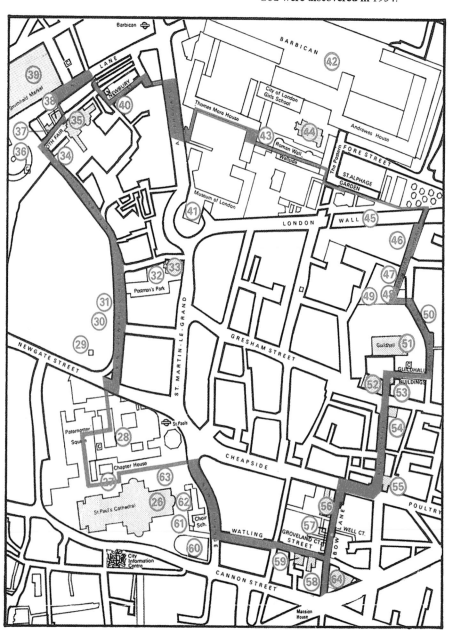

London Guildhall is where the Lord Mayor of the City of London and his sheriffs are elected.

The splendid St Paul's Cathedral built by Wren and completed in 1710.

The Barbican Arts centre is the largest in Europe and includes a concert hall, arts theatre, a School of Music and Drama and the Museum of London.

1. Start from St Paul's Cathedral, the Gothic masterpiece of the architect Sir Christopher Wren completed 1710. The central lantern is 111 metres high and it is one of the most famous in the world.

2. Follow the west Church Yard and on your right is the Chapter House, c1712. Built by Wren it survived the bombing of 1940.

3. Paternoster Square, a plaza of resting places, with shops and conveniences. Until 1869 it was a market for selling mutton, veal, pork and poultry

4. Step down and cross Newgate Street into King Edward Street. The National Postal Museum is on your left, founded in 1965.

5. The second oldest church in London St Bartholomew the Great, 1123 AD and St Bartholomew Hospital.

6. At the end of King Edward Street you can detour to Smithfield Market, the world's largest meat market.

7. Walk back along Little Britain following the road left to St Martin-le-Grand. St Botolph Church at Aldersgate was founded around 1291 and rebuilt 1791.

8. At the roundabout in Alders Gate is the headquarters of the Ironmongers Livery Company established as a craft fellowship in the 13th century.

9. Go up the steps to the Museum of London, which houses the greatest collections on the capital.

10. From the high walkway you can see the remains of a Roman Wall, built around 200 AD. It was 8m high, 3.2 km long and 2.4m thick.

11. Following the marked walkway north you reach the Barbican Centre which is open daily and contains a theatre, restaurant, art gallery, cinemas, library, sculpture court, Barbican Hall and lakeside terrace.

12. St Giles Cripplegate Church built 1390 has connections with Milton, Defoe and Frobisher.

13. St Alphage Church. Step down from end of London Wall walkway into Coleman Street and turn right into Basinghall Avenue.

14. The Guildhall, dating back to 1411, is the seat of the Corporation of London and the centre of city officials for over 800 years. The Great Hall has been the site of famous trials including Lady Jane Grey and Archbishop Crammer.

15. St Mary-le-Bow church, famous for its Bow Bells. East London Cockneys are those born within their sounds. Built in 1683 by Wren, it contains a Norman Crypt, believed to be the oldest ecclesiastical landmark in London.

16. Mansion House, erected in 1799, is the official residence of the Lord Mayor of the City of London.

17. Turn into King William Street to see the Bank of England, c1788, the Royal Exchange dating back to Elizabethan times and the London Stock Exchange.

18. Off King William Street in Monument Street stands the fine 17th century hollow fluted column, the Monument, by Wren.

19. Turn left into Lower Thames Street. On the riverside are Billingsgate, the former fish market, and the Custom House, former Port of London Customs headquarters.

20. All Hallows by the Tower Church has remains of a 7-8th century Saxon church and traces of a Roman temple dedicated to Mithras.

21. Tower of London, the 900 year-old Medieval fortress houses the Crown Jewels and armouries and is a top attraction for tourists.

22. Tower Hill Pageant, London's dark ride museum on capital's history.

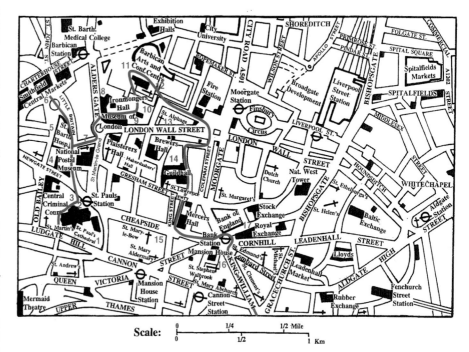

Scale:

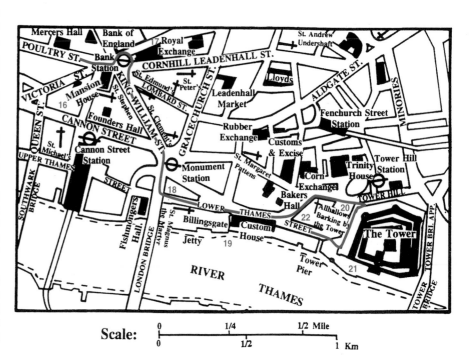

Scale:

Top: The Guildhall has been the City seat of government for 800 years. It contains an excellent reference library, founded in 1420, and a bookshop. Inset: The tall Monument. Right: The old Billingsgate Fish Market, c1876, and the adjacent former Customs House. Top right: The Museum of London has the greatest social collection on the Capital.

Within three months of the Battle of Hastings in 1066, William the Conqueror ordered the building of the White Tower of London, completed 1078, to create a building which was awe inspiring to people and frightening enough to keep them in their places!

The headquarters of the Ironmongers Livery Company in Alders Gate, was established during the 13th century.

East London Spitalfields

Walking around Spitalfields may be started from Aldgate tube station and could last about two hours. There are many excellent examples of 18th century weavers' houses. In 1888 the daily newspapers circulated gruesome reports of Jack the Ripper's murders in Spitalfields and Whitechapel but the mystery still continues.

1 Whitechapel Art Gallery opened in 1901. It contains paintings and sculptures from artists working in East London. Next, turn left into Middlesex Street.

2 Petticoat Lane is a world-famous market selling clothing, leather goods and jewellery.

3 Synagogue which was a French Protestant Church from 1766 and altered in the 19th century for its present use.

4 Artillery Lane where Nos 56 and 58 date back to early 18th century.

5 Walk northwards to Brushfield Street. No 52 is an early 18th century building. The cast iron lamp standard at the corner of Gun Street shows a relief of St Martin and the beggar.

6 Turn left into Commercial Street you see Christ Church and a large number of surviving 18th century houses along Fournier Street. Note the weaving attics with their long windows. No 2, "The Minster's House" was built by the architect, Hawksmoor.

7 On the west side of Commercial Street is Spitalfields Market. The fruit and vegetable market has been moved. Currently it has craft shops, stalls and restaurants.

8 Puma Court has the last surviving weaver's houses in the area.

9 In Spital Square, is the headquarters of the Society for Protection of Ancient Buildings, c1740.

10 Folgate Street is paved with 19th century setts. No 18, built 1724, was the home of silk weavers until 1919 and has been preserved.

11 Elder Street is a conservation area with many houses built from 1720.

12 From Commercial Street turn into Wheler Street and turn right into Bethnal Green Road. Turn right again and walk along Sclater Street until you reach Brick Lane Market. Brick Lane is lined with general stores and has many fine Bangladeshi and Indian restaurants. Carry on and cross Quaker Street and on your left is Brick Lane Music Hall.

13 Spitalfields Heritage Centre occupies a former Huguenot silk weaver's house dating from 1718.

14 Nearby is the Brick Lane Mosque for the Moslem community

15 Turn left into Hanbury Street and follow the map until you reach Whitechapel Road where you turn right. The Blind Beggar Pub has been the scene of both murder and salvation. This is the site where Ronnie Kray shot his arch-enemy George Cornell in 1966. In contrast, the pub marks the birth of the Salvation Army. Today the pub is a peaceful place to quench your thirst after a long walk.

16 Whitechapel Bell Foundry founded in 1570 and has occupied the present building since 1720. Bells found in many English churches and the American Liberty Bell were cast here.

Return to Aldgate station for your next destination or Central London.

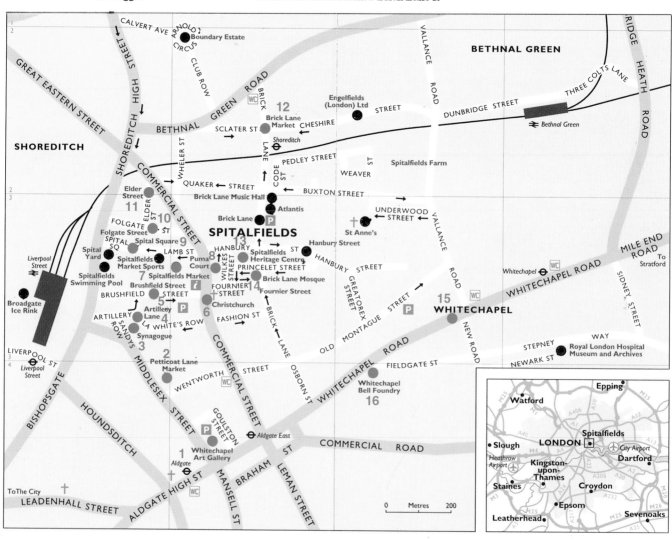

Brick Lane has small multi-culture shops for clothing, crafts, shoes, leather goods and Indian food.

The 69m high spire of Christ Church dominates the neighbourhood.

Brick Lane Mosque is used by the Bangladeshi community. It was built originally as Huguenot weavers' school and chapel and then passed to Methodist.

In Old Spitalfields Market you find craft shops, restaurants, sport and art activities.

Spitalfields is well known for its curry houses, mainly Bangladeshi and Indian cuisine.

Historic Riverside Walk

In 1613, Sir Hugh Myddelton, a goldsmith in the City of London, successfully completed the construction of the 'New River', which was a channel 3m wide, on average 1.2m deep and almost 64 km long. This brought water from Chadwell Springs in Hertfordshire to the Round Pond and New River Head building in Islington. The water was stored in a reservoir and distributed by a system of wooden and lead pipes to the City of London. King James I was Myddelton's partner in the enterprise and owned half the shares in the New River Company. The New River was needed because of the dreadful state of London's water supply up to the end of the 16th century. In 1688 the New River Head witnessed the opening of Sadlers Wells nearby, which started as a centre of healing and music and today in their new building is an important theatre for British opera and ballet.

The following historic walk is a trail of the river in its hey day. Further information is provided in the map and illustrations.

1   New River source at Chadwell Springs near Ware in Hertfordshire.
2   New Gauge, the intake for the New River at King's Mead near Hertford.
3   The old Foot Bridge at Amwell Pond, Hertfordshire.
4   Turnford Pumping Station, near Chesthunt.
5   The New River flowing alongside Theobalds Park.
6   The Sluice House at Enfield Town.
7   The Stone at Chadwell Springs, the source of the New River in Hertfordshire, inscribed with date and detail of New River works.
8   Pumping Station in Hornsey, North London.
9   The "Castle" Pumping Station at Green Lanes in Stoke Newington, North London.
10 The old Engine Room of the Pumping Station, Stoke Newington.
11 The old New River Head and Round Pond at Clerkenwell in London.

When the New River company was taken over by the Metropolitan Water Board in 1904, it was supplying 1¼million people with 40million gallons of water per day. The Round Pond was abandoned in 1914 and the New Head building was occupied later by Thames Water created in 1974. It was sold recently for conversion into private apartments.

The New River today ends at Green Lanes, Stoke Newington, but a section of it is preserved as ornamental gardens in Islington

and this provides the following relaxing walk. The rest of the river is not accessible except in short lengths in parks and open spaces, for example in Finsbury Park.

New River Walk Today at Islington

a   Start at Canonbury BR station and walk south along Wallace Road.
b   Cross St Paul's Road and the New River Walk of 2.4km (1½ miles) is signposted and runs parallel to Douglas Road and Canonbury Grove.
c   At the end of the walk turn right into Canonbury Road and right again into Essex Road.
d   Near the junction of Essex Road and Colebrooke Row you will see Charles Lamb's house and the Statue of Sir Hugh Myddelton at Islington Green.
e   At Angel tube station, fork right into St John Street and the New River Head buildings on your right. It contains the magnificent Oak Room.

North of Stoke Newington, the New River is still an open channel with well kept grassy banks, parts of which can be walked along, playing fields and parks clearly marked on London maps. A good view of the river can be seen in Oakthorpe Road, Palmers Green.

1. New River Source, Chadwell Springs, Ware.
2. New Gauge, King's Mead, Hertford.
3. Foot Bridge, Amwell Pond, Herts.
4. Turnford Pumping-Station, Cheshunt.
5. Theobalds Park.
6. Sluice House, Enfield.
7. Hornsey Pumping-Station.
8. Stone at Chadwell Springs, inscribed with date of New River works.
9. Pumping-Station, Green Lanes, Stoke Newington.
10. Engine-room of Pumping-Station.
11. New River Head, Clerkenwell.

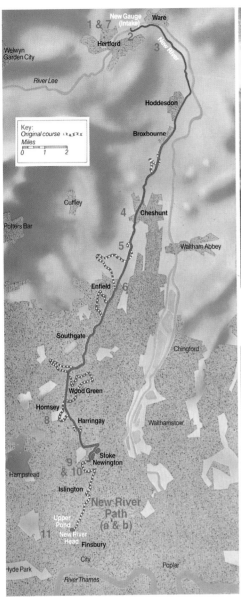

The current map showing the New River and River Lee.

Portrait of King James I, who put up half the money towards the cost of building the New River between 1609 and 1613.

Sir Hugh Myddelton, who built the scheme, was a Hatten Garden Jeweller.

Top: The New Gauge, intake for the New River. Right: The "Castle" - pumping station at Stoke Newington where the New River ends today.

Top: "Sir Hugh Myddelton Glory", an engraving of the opening ceremony in 1613 when water was let into the Round Pond at Islington. Myddelton is standing next to his horse on the right.

Right: A picture of the 400-year old New River, which during the new millennium is a key to the recharge of chalk aquifer in North London by pumping water into it from the river. The insets show the plan for the scheme and one of the new pumping stations, c1999.

London Eye - Millennium Wheel

The Millennium Wheel, known as the London Eye, is one of three spectacular attractions to celebrate the New Millennium in London, the other two are the Millennium Dome in North Greenwich and the Millennium Footbridge at Bankside. This latest addition to London's skyline takes people on an half hour ride above the Thames. The £30million project took about a year to build and from the top, on a clear day, passengers are able to see as far as a 40km radius around London.

The wheel has been built in the Jubilee Gardens on the South Bank, next to the former Greater London County Hall. The nearest tube stations are Westminster and Waterloo. Components for the 1600 tonne structure were fabricated throughout Europe including tubular steel for the rim from British Steel, cables from Italy and the central spindle from a Czech company, better known for their cars, Skoda. The wheel was constructed horizontally on barges across half the width of the Thames, and then raised into a vertical position by giant cranes.

As a structure it is huge, the fourth tallest in London. In capacity, it is the world's highest observation wheel. Sponsored by British Airways, the London Eye, is a structure without parallel. It is the biggest Ferris wheel in the world, with an overall diameter of 135m to the outside of the passenger capsules. The 32 capsules, each carrying 25 people, offer a bird's eye view of London during each rotation. A view of the capsules being transported along the Thames is shown opposite.

Most Ferris wheels are supported from both sides of the hub and spindle, whereas the London Eye is cantilevered out from the river's edge. A spindle surrounded by the hub goes through the centre of the wheel, supported from the riverbank by an A-shaped frame. The spindle is equivalent in height to a 7-storey building when stood on its end.

The wheel has a steel rim and forces are transmitted to the central hub through 75 spokes attached to nodes. The weight of the wheel is supported from the spokes. The wheel works like a bicycle wheel. The wheel and hub turn on bearings around a fixed spindle, driven by a motor with wheels that run against the rim. The A-frame essentially works like one of the forks on a bicycle supporting the structure off the ground. Enjoy your ride!

Views of landmarks and attractions seen from the wheel are shown on the opposite page.

Top: Houses of Parliament, Westminster Abbey, White Hall with St James's Park in the background. Left: Aerial view of the south bank of River Thames from Waterloo Bridge to Canary Wharf, also showing the City waterfront.

Top: Bird's eye view of Tower Bridge, the Tower of London and the City looking north. Left: The River Thames and its embankments looking south, from Royal Festival Hall to Battersea Power Station, showing the London Eye, Millennium wheel.

Top: The New Shakespeare Theatre and the New Tate Gallery for modern art, which are connected to St Pauls by the new Millennium Footbridge. Right: The Millennium Dome on the Greenwich Peninsula, as seen from the air in February 2000.

Acknowledgements

I am deeply indebted to previous writers, numerous individuals, photographers, estate agents and many diverse organisations whose information helped greatly with the preparation of this book. I would like to express my thanks to my institution, the University of East London, for its support of the research over many years. For the supply of much information and maps, I am deeply grateful to the former London Docklands Development Corporation (LDDC) and the Port of London Authority (PLA). Appreciation and acknowledgement must be made to Mr Peter Marsh of the Financial Times, who was commissioned by the LDDC to produce walks in five map leaflets. Thanks are also due to Colin Hynson and Osman Streater.

To Canary Wharf Development Company and Olympia & York special thanks are given for the supply of photographs and maps. For the supply of aerial photographs I am most grateful to Chorley and Handford,

Surrey. The assistance and co-operation of Tom Samson and Paul Proctor are very much appreciated. Acknowledgement with thanks has to be made for information received previously from the Museum of London and the Museum of Docklands.

I would like to thank sincerely Linda Day for her help, excellent typing and patience in preparation of the whole manuscript with great care. I am grateful to Terence O'Connell for general assistance and to George Cossey for his kind reviews. Special thanks are due to Tom Juffs for his enthusiasm and unstinting support throughout. I would like to express my deep gratitude to Dr John Grubert for proof reading and assistance with the layout. I am grateful to Dr Paul Smith for advice and to Joyce O'Neill for typing, co-operation and her continued help. Thanks are due to Dave Hobson and his staff at Lipscomb Printers. I am most grateful to my wife, Irene, for her support and patience over many years.

Information was obtained from many organisations including Docklands News, Meridian Magazine, Port of London Magazine, New Civil Engineer, Readers Digest, Butlers Wharf Limited, St Martins Property Corporation, Colin Druce, Docklands Light Railway, the Daily Telegraph, Evening Standard, Daily Mirror, The Times, Savilles Property, Prudential Property, Carleton Smith, Clapshaws, Cluttons, Shakespeare Globe Theatre and Millennium Experience Company,

To members of the public, visitors, students, teachers and scholars world-wide, who have kindly supported our book publications over the past two decades, some of which are in their seventh and eighth editions, I express my deepest appreciation. The books are standard texts in schools and colleges and are providing an essential public service.

Information

A unique set of nine internationally acknowledged research books have been published on the history, heritage, regeneration, infrastructure, walks and millennium of London and Docklands. They are ideal for teaching and research in schools and colleges as well as for libraries, visitors, the general public and walkers.

"London and Docklands Walks" The Explorer (ISBN 1-8745 36-25-2)
"London Water Heritage" Portrait in Words and Pictures (ISBN 1-8745-36-40-6),
"London Docklands" Past, Present and Future (ISBN 0-091987-81-6),
"Discover London Docklands" A-Z Illustrated Guide to Modern Docklands (ISBN 1-874536-00-7),
"European Docklands", Past, Present and Future (ISBN 0-901987-82-4),
"London Illustrated" Historical, Current and Future (ISBN 1-874536-01-5),
"London Docklands Guide" Heritage and Millennium Exhibition (ISBN 1-874536-03-1).
"London Millennium Guide" Education, Entertainment and Aspirations (ISBN 1-8745-36-20-1).
"Dockland" Historical Survey (ISBN 0-901987-8).

For further information visit the University of East London Web Site on
www.uel.ac.uk
or telephone 020 8223 2531,
Fax 020 8223 2963.

PLEASE ORDER THROUGH:
RESEARCH BOOKS,
P O. BOX 82,
ROMFORD, ESSEX,
RM8 2AS, GREAT BRITAIN